WHERE IS YOUR ALLEGIANCE?

THE MESSAGE TO THE SEVEN CHURCHES

PAUL HIMES

Energion Publicatiions
Gonzalez, Forida
2017

Copyright © Paul Himes 2017

Unless otherwise indicated, scripture references are taken from the King James Version, adapted by the author based on the source texts.

Scriptures marked NIV are taken from the Holy Bible, New International Version®, NIV®. Copyright © 1973, 1978, 1984, 2011 by Biblica, Inc.™ Used by permission of Zondervan. All rights reserved worldwide. www.zondervan.com The "NIV" and "New International Version" are trademarks registered in the United States Patent and Trademark Office by Biblica, Inc.™

Electronic Editions:
    Kindle: 978-1-63199-410-4
    Adobe e-Book: 978-1-63199-411-1
    Google Play ePub: 978-1-63199-412-8
    iBooks: 978-1-63199-413-5/

Print ISBNs:
ISBN10: 1-63199-409-3
ISBN13: 978-1-63199-409-8
Library of Congress Control Number: 2017945508

Energion Publications
P. O. Box 841
Gonzalez, FL 32560

energion.com
pubs@energion.com
850-525-3916

Dedication

To my youth Sunday School class at Bethany Hills Baptist Church (now Trinity Bible Church), Raleigh, NC, especially from 2013-2014
To Kevin Miner, for your friendship and support

Acknowledgments

I am immensely grateful for this opportunity to write on the Revelation of Jesus Christ. This book, first and foremost, owes everything to the eternal life found in Jesus the Messiah, the key figure of Revelation and of all the cosmos. To him alone be my highest praise for ever and ever!

Secondly, I wish to dedicate this book to all the young men and women who were in my youth Sunday School class over at Bethany Hills Baptist Church (now Trinity Bible Church). This book is the direct result of our Revelation study from Fall 2013 to Spring 2014. Your interest, discussion, and excellent questions are what spurred me on to write this book, and I am immensely grateful. May you place the Lamb first in your lives!

Next, I wish to thank Kevin Miner for his friendship all these years. I view Kevin as an excellent paradigm for a layperson in the church, one who can study Scripture for himself and teach others, without ever being ordained. Your own research and teaching on Laodicea puts you a step above the majority of Baptist preachers I've heard on the topic!

For proofreading and suggestions on style and content, I am grateful for my father John R. Himes, and Zack and Jessica Reed. Thanks for all your help!

Finally, I wish to thank the publishers of Energion, Henry and Jody Neufeld, for taking a chance on a rookie (this is my first work intended for the broader Christian audience rather than academia)! I greatly appreciate Energion's focus on publishing for Christians outside of the academy's ivory towers, and I pray that my book will provide a helpful contribution to their mission. In addition, I am grateful to Chris Eyre at Energion for editorial corrections and suggestions.

Table of Contents

Acknowledgments iv

1 Seven Churches and Their Rightful King 1
2 Introducing the Lamb 9
3 Christians In The Shadow Of Empire 29
4 Ephesus — Losing Your First Love 49
5 Smyrna—Fear Not the Persecutor 63
6 Pergamum—Whose Banquet Are You Attending? 75
7 Thyatira—Beware the Rogue Prophetess 85
8 Sardis—The Vulnerable Fortress 97
9 Philadelphia—Longing for a City With no Earthquakes 105
10 Laodicea—Self-Sufficient Churches
    Make Jesus Want To Puke 117
11 How Should We Respond? 129

Resources for Further Study 135
Bibliography 139

1

Seven Churches and Their Rightful King

The bleak fortress of Sardis jutted up against the overcast sky as a smattering of rain fell on the Greco-Syrian soldiers beneath. While the besiegers shivered, cold and damp, the citadel's Anatolian defenders complacently gazed at their enemy below, confident that this was one city that could not be conquered by force of arms.

Nearby, King Antiochus III watched the foreboding citadel, contemplating. No longer young and inexperienced, the Greco-Syrian king was in the process of carving out a significant slice of the Middle East for himself. Although he had also experienced recent defeat at the hands of the Egyptian king, Ptolemy IV Philopater, Antiochus was basically at the height of his power and would reign supreme throughout Syria, ancient Persia, and even to the very borders of India itself, not to mention Asia Minor. Eventually, stylizing himself as a "defender" of the freedom of the Greek people groups against the ascendant Roman Empire, he would learn that talk is cheap, subsequently becoming one more statistic, just another king crushed under Rome's imperial boot.

Yet now, in 213 BC, putting aside his ambitions towards Egypt, Antiochus III has had time to consolidate his empire and chase his rebellious cousin Archaeus all the way to Sardis. His cousin's fate is sealed—before the conflict is over, Archaeus will die a most gruesome death.

Before that can happen, though, the intimidating fortress of Sardis will have to be dealt with. This leviathan of defense was surrounded by sheer cliffs on three sides; the only access point was a narrow, easily-defendable ridge, called the "Saw," jagged pieces of rock jutting out menacingly, connecting the fortress to the city below.

Yet even as Antiochus bleakly considered the impossibility of taking the fortress by anything other than famine, he was approached by the old veteran from Crete, Lagoras. Lagoras told him that he had been observing the Saw, and noticed that many vultures and other carrion congregated there, indicating a lack of guards. Quite possibly the area would be accessible by a few elite men with ladders, who could then reach the gate itself, opening it for the rest of the army.

Antiochus agreed, and the plan was hatched. Waiting for a moonless night, Lagoras requisitioned the burly Theodotus of Anatolia and Dionysius, the tough leader of the king's bodyguard itself, together with fifteen other elite men. This band of eighteen would climb the Saw and attack the gate from the inside, timed to coincide with an assault by thirty men attempting to break through the gate from the outside.

The evening finally came, and the plan was put into motion. The ladders were virtually invisible to the Anatolian defenders, due to the lack of soldiers guarding The Saw itself, but Lagoras had not counted on the noisy surprise of his own army once the ladders went up in full view of the camp. Thinking quickly, Antiochus sent a significant force to attack the gate farthest away from Lagoras' ninja-like infiltration, successfully drawing away the enemy's attention. Lagoras' band crested the Saw, dropped down onto the path below, slaughtered the startled Anatolian defenders, and began sawing through the gate (as those outside did the same). Within a short time, Antiochus' army was through the gate and swarming over the outer defenses of Sardis. Massacres, fires, and looting soon followed.[1]

---

1 This is my own retelling of the story based on Polybius, *Histories*, book 7, Chapters 15–17 (trans. W. R. Paton), with some background information taken from Grant R. Osborne, *Revelation*, BECNT (Grand Rapids, MI: Baker Academic, 2002), 171.

The great fortress of Sardis, virtually impenetrable to conventional arms, for the second time in its history had fallen to a sneak attack. Elite soldiers had entered through an unexpected avenue, like house burglars through a carelessly opened window, aided by the lack of vigilance of those responsible for protecting the city.

Now, almost 300 years later, Sardis is approached by a different King. This one, though, does not approach as a conqueror besieging a captive people. To the contrary, he is already their rightful Lord; he has won their allegiance through the shedding of his blood and mighty resurrection from the dead. Inexplicably, though, the people seem unaware of the presence of their own King. Consequently, Jesus himself warns the church at Sardis that, if necessary, he will come to them "as a thief in the night" (3:3), just like Lagoras centuries before. One way or the other, the church at Sardis will bow before her King.

Reading Somebody Else's Mail

For each church mentioned in Revelation, the history and background of their respective cities plays a significant role in Jesus' letters to them. In each case, Jesus has tailored a very personal epistle to a very specific audience, occasionally including very confrontational material, generally not the sort of material one would want exposed to the public. He is, in essence, "airing [the] churches' dirty laundry."[1] Nevertheless, at the end of each letter, Jesus declares, "Whoever has an ear, listen to what the Spirit says to the churches!"[2] In other words, Jesus intends for all Christians,

---

1 Ben Witherington III, *Revelation*, NCBC (Cambridge: Cambridge University Press, 2003), 109.
2 All translations, unless otherwise noted, are my own updating of the King James, with slight modification, under consultation with the following Greek texts: 1. Stephanus' 1550 edition of the *Textus Receptus* (compiled by Maurice Robinson); 2. The *Novum Testamentum Graecae* (Nestle-Aland) 27th ed.; and 3. *The New Testament in the Original Greek: Byzantine Textform 2005* (Robinson-Pierpont). The first two texts were accessed via *Accordance* 11.1.6 (OakTree Software, 2016). In addition, at times I have consulted and cited the *The Holy Bible: New International Version*

of every era, every ethnicity, and every temperament, to listen in on these private conversations and learn from them.

Each of those seven churches is addressed in such a way that no doubt exists about who holds the true power in the world—not Rome, not the local authorities, not any pagan gods, but Jesus Christ the Jewish Messiah, Savior of the World. As the true Lord of the world (rather than Caesar), he speaks in language that demands ultimate allegiance from each Christian and each church. In other words, Jesus Christ does not approach his church with hat in hand, humbly begging for an audience. Rather, he overwhelms them with the force of his Being, directly confronting them about any spiritual flaws he sees.

In fact, as Alan Bandy argues, one can even see a type of "prophetic lawsuit" in these chapters, hearkening back to the "covenant lawsuit imagery" of the Old Testament prophets.[1] Bandy further stresses the "forensic," or "judicial" nature of these letters: Jesus Christ portrays himself as one who "wields judicial authority" and also functions as the one acting out the "judicial investigations" regarding the character of the Christians who are accountable to him.[2] In two cases, Jesus' forensic investigation yields positive results: those churches are worthy of praise and serve as models for others. In three instances, Jesus' investigation yields mixed results: some of the church's actions pass the test, while other parts need reform. For two other churches, the verdict is nothing but negative.

Yet Jesus is a fair judge, and in the midst of his harshness he nonetheless offers hope for the repentant. In other words, in the court that decides a church's status, although the verdict may be "guilty," the punishment is not yet given until a church (and each individual Christian) has had a chance to repent. In one, possibly two cases in Revelation 2–3, the potential punishment seems to be

---

(Colorado Springs, CO: Biblica, 1973), accessed from https://www.blueletterbible.org. This will be noted in the text.

1 Alan S. Bandy, "Patterns of Prophetic Lawsuits in the Oracles to the Seven Churches," *Neotestamentica* 45.2 (2011): 179–180.
2 Ibid., 196–197.

the extinction of the local church itself (Ephesus definitely, and Pergamum maybe). However, even in these instances the local church is given more than enough time to change.

These first three chapters of Revelation, then, are primarily about Jesus Christ and his church. While Revelation does contain prophecy, too often we have focused on the eschatology of Revelation at the near exclusion of its Christology and ecclesiology. While eschatology (what will happen in the future) is certainly important, the main message of Revelation is *not* "let's match up this book with current events" but rather "Jesus is Lord, and he is coming back, so act like it!" In fact, I would offer the following challenge to the reader (and to myself): one cannot begin to grapple with the eschatology of Revelation until one has submitted to the Christology of Revelation. Granted, who Jesus Christ is remains inseparably linked to the fact that he is coming back—his Messianic role demands it! My point, however, is that we must come face to face with who Jesus is, and submit to him as such, *before* grappling with when he is coming back, the nature of the Millennium, or the myriad of interpretive issues in the remainder of this book. Furthermore, ultimately the test of one's spirituality is *not* one's views on how Revelation matches up with current (or past) events, but rather whether or not one has submitted to Jesus as Lord.

This book, then, is first and foremost a discussion of the One who addresses the seven churches, and what we can learn from his message to them. Only by understanding Jesus Christ can we hope to understand the message of Revelation. In addition, the more we discuss the One who speaks to the Anatolian churches, the more we realize that he demands something that nobody else, neither man nor spirit nor nation, can have: our wholehearted allegiance at the exclusion of all other competitors. Jesus Christ, and him alone, demands the church's reverence; compromising by offering obeisance to the emperor, the empire, or local pagan gods results in the harshest censure from the King of Kings.

In other words, Revelation ultimately asks the following question: *who or what really has our allegiance?* Rome, the emperor, and local pagan deities all clamored for attention from the harassed Anatolian Christians; capitulating by offering allegiance and reverence to such entities would make their life easier. Yet the Church's identity has always been inextricably linked to how Christians view Jesus—not as merely another divine or semi-divine being worthy of worship, but as *the only Name* that accomplishes salvation and thus *the only human* worthy of reverence and total allegiance. Indeed, since all nations will be forced to bow the knee before Jesus in the end, consequently how "unbelievably foolish ... for those who are part of the people of God to surrender their legacy in favor of entering allegiances, real or virtual, with Rome"[1] (or, I might add, any modern nation or entity).

This book will examine the first three chapters of Revelation, paying special attention to the background of each city as well as the major theological themes in both Revelation's presentation of Jesus Christ and Jesus' message to the seven churches. I hope that this book will be useful to Christians, regardless of eschatological orientation—Dispensational, Reformed, and everybody in between!

Having said that, my own perspective on the seven churches disagrees with the so-called "historical" view that equates each of them with some era in church history. In my opinion, this reads too much into the text, assuming an interpretation that no 1st–2nd century Christian could possibly have conceived of. Furthermore, if pushed too far, the equation of the seven churches with seven historical eras results in a disturbingly Anglo-centric view that, for example, by equating "lukewarm Laodicea" with the church today, ignores the suffering churches in such places as India, China, and Muslim nations (churches that may resemble Smyrna more than Laodicea). Rather, just like any other church mentioned in the New Testament, each of these seven churches contains lessons for *all* ages.

---

1 Allan J. McNicol, *The Conversion of the Nations in Revelation*, LNTS 438 (London: T&T Clark, 2011), 106.

This is not to say, however, that the seven churches do not have some deeper symbolic meaning. The number "seven" occurs an incredible 30-31 times [depending on one's Greek NT] in the book of Revelation, roughly half the occurrences of the entire New Testament! Seven Spirits, seven churches seven angels, seven trumpets, etc., etc.—regardless of how one interprets the book, the recurrence of this number is significant and quite often (though not always) associated with objects that are of divine origin (notice, however, the Great Counterfeiter's seven heads and seven crowns in Revelation 12:3). Thus, although we take the "seven churches" to refer to seven literal and historical churches, we nonetheless acknowledge that the number seven was not chosen randomly but resonates with a broader theme in Revelation.

On the practical side, I must offer one caution before we proceed: as we examine the seven churches of Revelation 2–3, the point is *not* to sit in judgment upon our own local church, and wish they were a little less like Laodicea (or whatever). The point is to *first* sit in judgment upon our own selves (Matthew 7:3–5), beg the Lord to conform us to the image of Jesus Christ, and *only then* will we be in a position to enact change, not with a judgmental, "holier-than-though" attitude, but from a chastened and humble perspective that points people to Jesus Christ, not to ourselves.

Finally, the oft-neglected third member of the Trinity, the Holy Spirit, plays a major role in these seven epistles. In fact, Jesus' words are portrayed consistently as what the Spirit says to the churches. No study of Revelation can succeed in strengthening our faith and conforming us to the image of Jesus Christ unless the Holy Spirit is involved. So, my fellow Christian, as you crack open this most puzzling of books (Revelation, that is; not mine!), ask for the Spirit's guidance; I guarantee he will be a better guide than my book or any other commentary.

2 INTRODUCING THE LAMB

"Christology is the heart of the matter for John ..."
(Ben Witherington III)[1]

Before we can figure out *what* Revelation is about, we first must understand *who* it is about. At first glance, this might seem like a stupid question; yet my own experience has shown me that the "Jesus" of many an American is hardly the Jesus of Revelation, but rather a BFF who never demands anything and only gives. Jesus basically helps them out of tight spots, offers soothing words of encouragement, and gives them direction to a better life. In other words, "Jesus" = Pikachu, Mr. Rogers, and Siri all rolled into one.

Yet the above description cannot begin to accurately portray the Being who confronts us in Revelation, and if we misunderstand Jesus in Revelation's first chapter, we misunderstand all of Revelation. The Jesus of Revelation is (to borrow from C. S. Lewis), not a "safe" Jesus. He is not the happily smiling, warm and fuzzy Jesus of pop-culture who only occasionally pings "FaceTime" for our attention and "likes" all our posts on Facebook.

Granted, on the one hand the Jesus of Revelation is still our best friend, full of the love of God, the same merciful, compassionate Jewish Messiah who healed the sick and made the lame to walk in Galilee. We do not, however, have the right to accept only the parts of Jesus that do not frighten us. To paraphrase Augustine, "If you believe what you like about Jesus, and reject what you don't like, it is not Jesus you are believing in but yourself." The Jesus of

---

1   Witherington, *Revelation*, 27.

Revelation overwhelms us with his magnificence, demands our obedience, and warns us of the consequences if we ignore him. He is nothing less than the Sovereign Lord of the universe.

This chapter, then, is about the Jesus of Revelation, especially as John portrays him in Revelation 1. We will not be very motivated to take seriously the warnings and promises of Chapters 2–3 if we do not first take seriously the Lord Jesus Christ, in all his kingly magnificence.

John's Description of Jesus

The Jesus of John's Apocalypse is, first of all, located within the Trinity. John's epistolary introduction in 1:4-5 points us to the Father ("from him who is, and who was, and who is to come"), the Spirit ("the Seven Spirits," or, perhaps "the seven-fold Spirit")[1] and Jesus Christ. Surprisingly, though, John was not content with simply asserting that Jesus was united with the Father and Spirit. He proceeds to focus exclusively on the Son in this prologue; while the Father and the Spirit obviously play key roles here, Jesus Christ is the one who takes center stage.

Furthermore, the language used to describe Jesus Christ in Revelation is deliberately parallel to the language used to describe the Father. The result is that, even though distinction is maintained (e.g., 19:15; significantly, the Father is the only one called "*pantokratōr*," or "All-powerful"), John's language sometimes blurs the line between Father and Son. For example, 1:8 sees the Father declaring himself to be "the Alpha and the Omega" while in 1:17 we see the Son declaring himself to be the "First and the Last."[2] The Father, on the one hand, is "the one who is and the one who was and the one who is coming" (1:4) while the Son is "the one

---

[1] For a discussion on the nature of the "seven Spirits" in this passage, drawing from Isaiah 11:2 LXX and Zechariah 4:2-10, see Osborne, *Revelation*, 61 and 74-75.
[2] Richard Bauckham, *The Theology of the Book of Revelation*, NTT (Cambridge: Cambridge University Press, 1993), 54–55.

living, who was dead, and is living forever" (1:18) and who will also "come with the clouds" (1:7).

Jesus as the Witness

Significantly, John starts us off with Jesus Christ as "the faithful witness," a theme that, in a sense, blankets the entire book. Revelation opens with John identifying himself as one who "witnessed" (Greek *martureō*) Jesus Christ, and closes with the same Greek word used three times in 22:16–20, as both Jesus and John "testify" or "witness" to the validity and sacredness of all that has been written. In one sense, the question "Who is God's witness?" brackets the entire book of Revelation.

Because Jesus himself is the ultimate "witness" or "testimony," so believers, as well, are to be a testimony. In fact, almost exactly in the middle of the book, Revelation 12:11, Christian martyrs are said to have overcome Satan through "the blood of the Lamb, and the word of their *testimony*" (Greek *martus*).[1] This is barely the tip of the iceberg—Revelation is full of references to "witness/testimony"; in fact, this particular Greek word group (*martus* and similar words) occurs a total of 16 times in Revelation, demonstrating how important this term is (only Acts and the Gospel of John, fittingly, use these words more frequently).

So in what way is Jesus Himself the "witness" or "testifier"? Richard Bauckham, in his classic theological work on Revelation, declares that this title "refers primarily to the witness which Jesus bore to God during his life on earth and to his faithfulness in maintaining his witness even at the cost of his life."[2] Jesus, then, points all creation to God—indeed, the key purpose of the incarnation was to point to God (John 1:18)! Consequently, Jesus' own act of

---

[1] As Frank S. Thielman aptly states, "By means of the Lamb's blood and their own perseverance within a social environment hostile to their faith, Christians are able to prevail over the accusations of Satan" ("The Atonement," in *Central Themes in Biblical Theology: Mapping Unity in Diversity* [Grand Rapids, MI: Baker Academic, 2007], 123).

[2] Bauckham, *Theology of Revelation*, 72.

testifying of God becomes the model for all believers, even to the point of death; the ultimate model Christian, as far as Revelation is concerned, is Antipas (2:13), described in near-identical terms to Jesus himself: "my faithful one, my witness." Just as Jesus Himself points to God, even to the point of death (Philippians 2:8), so also the followers of Jesus must "witness" or "testify" of God, even if it costs their life (Revelation 2:10).

In other words, the act of "testifying" or "witnessing" is a key function of both Jesus Christ and his followers in Revelation.[1] Truth cannot be known without witnesses. Just as the absence of witnesses in a court of law may lead to the suppression of the truth (e.g., nobody will ever learn who broke into the bank, or how), so the lack of witness to the goodness and justice of God in this world will suppress the truth. Granted, the universe itself can act as a witness, in a sense (Psalm 19); yet what Jesus especially desires are *organic* witnesses who, like him, can point humanity to the glory and mercy of God. This, indeed, is a major reason for Israel and the Law's existence (Deuteronomy 4:5–8, Psalm 67), as well as the Church's existence (1 Peter 2:9).

We see, then, that just as Jesus points to the Father in word and deed, so also must believers. I say "word" and "deed" because both of these types of "witness/testimony" are emphasized in Revelation as well as the rest of the New Testament. On the one hand, the testimony of Jesus Christ is meant to be proclaimed *vocally*, beginning with the reading of the seven letters themselves and closing out with the direct invitation by the Spirit and the Bride to anyone who might be listening (22:17—"the one who hears" extends the invitation of the Spirit and the Bride to anybody desiring eternal life). This theme of vocal "testimony" reaches its peak in Revelation 7:9–12, where an enormous, ethnically diverse group shouts praises to both the Father and the Lamb. Interestingly, the author portrays this as the incredible honor given specifically to

---

[1] For an excellent discussion of the theme of "witness" in connection to the "courtroom" and "judge" motif in Revelation, see Bauckham, *Theology of Revelation*, 72–73, and 105.

those who had suffered through a great time of tribulation. They are given the privilege of *witnessing* on the cosmic stage because they had *witnessed* by giving their lives on the earthly stage, due to their confession of the Name.[1] Furthermore, it is doubtful that John himself would have been exiled to Patmos "because of the witness of [i.e., about] Jesus Christ" if he, personally, had never mentioned the name of Jesus out loud.

On the other hand, Revelation focuses a lot on "works" or "deeds," especially when Jesus is addressing the seven churches. Vocal proclamation without a Jesus-centered life will be counter-productive to God's kingdom. As we shall see, some of the seven churches were actually harming their testimony through syncretism—believers were claiming the name of Jesus, but at the same time offering reverence to pagan gods and the Roman emperor.

Through Revelation, then, we believers are called to "witness," not spend our time twiddling our thumbs and doing nothing in anticipation of Jesus' return. I believe G. K. Beale is absolutely correct in pointing us to the pastoral message, the *imperative*, of Revelation: "The focus of the book is exhortation to the church community to witness to Christ in the midst of a compromising, idolatrous church and world."[2]

Unfortunately, it is easy for those living in an affluent and tolerant nation to become too easily content and boastful of the extent of their "witness," as if an occasional tract or personal testimony is sufficient. Yet, as mentioned above, the ultimate "witness" to God is the act of laying down one's life (making Antipas in Revelation 2:13 the "model witness"). Consequently, North American Christianity has no claim to being the best example of "witness." In an era where Asian and African Christians, especially, are more likely to suffer (socially and physically) for the cause of Jesus Christ, the

---

1 See Bauckham, *Theology of Revelation*, 84, on the significance of their witness and its consequences.
2 G. K. Beale, *The Book of Revelation*, NIGTC (Grand Rapids, MI: Eerdmans, 1999), 33.

time has come for American Christians to re-examine our own historical status.

Indeed, for years American Christians have claimed, even bragged, that "America" is a "Christian nation," simply on the basis of Christianity being the "norm." Yet if model Christianity is that which suffers persecution because it is anything *but* the norm within society, have we truly been accurate in our boasting? In other words, since Revelation portrays the "best Christians" on earth as those who *suffer* for Jesus Christ (just as Jesus himself suffered; see 1 Peter 2:19–25), and since this is *least* likely to be true in a nation where "Christianity" is culturally accepted, then we must conclude that most North American Christians generally cannot hold a candle to many of our Asian and African brothers and sisters when it comes to who, truly, exemplify the concept of "witness" as found in Revelation. There have been exceptions, of course; even America has seen religious persecution before, and North America may yet become hostile to Christianity. If so, we should welcome this change as an event that enables us to be better witnesses, rather than whining about the "good old days" when America was "a Christian nation" (Ecclesiastes 7:10).

In other words, the most valuable "witness" is that which *costs* something. Any form of Christianity that can only direct people to Jesus Christ from the comfort of their soft pews and heated sanctuaries, with no fear of persecution, is not wholly experiencing what it means to be a "witness."

Jesus the Resurrected One

Thus Christians, according to Revelation, are to "testify" to the One who himself "testifies" of God. Yet Jesus is not *merely* a witness for God. If this were the case, he would be no different from any of the prophets or even a good preacher. Jesus' uniqueness is predicated on, among other things, his designation as "Firstborn of the dead" (1:5). The terminology that Jesus is the "firstborn" indicates that he paves the way for a new class of people in the timeline of history; as Markus Barth points out, "The resurrection of Jesus Christ is presented as an event that *concludes one era and inaugurates another.*"[1]

This resurrection of the Messiah is at the heart of Revelation. Furthermore, this "resurrection" is not something that should be explained away in psychological or emotional terms, e.g., a warm and fuzzy "Jesus risen in my heart," an every-day, "normal" occurrence for Christians. Whatever is going on here, it is not "normal," explainable by either internal or psychological experience. Indeed, the very language here decisively mitigates all our attempts to suppress the scandal of the resurrection with "spiritual" terminology. If the "risen" Jesus were nothing more than an emotionally uplifting experience, then this would hardly qualify as a sign of the end of the age, or something that signifies the uniqueness of his claim to being the Jewish Messiah.[2] If Jesus, confronting the seven churches, cannot claim to have physically risen from the dead, then he has no basis for accusing them of spiritual idolatry when they worship other gods. After all, one can just as easily experience "Cybele risen in my heart" or "the gracious Caesar risen in my heart" as "Jesus risen in my heart"; to claim a physical resurrection, however, is to stake one's divine identity on a radically claim that can potentially be falsified but that, if true, vindicates the claimant.

In other words, whatever it means for Jesus Christ to be the "Firstborn of the dead"—to be "resurrected"—it *must* mean more than simply "appearing to others after death" (in a dream, as a ghost, or whatever).[3] It must mean the "reversal, the undoing, the conquest of death" by the possession of a physical body.[4] If Jesus

---

1 Markus Barth and Verne H. Fletcher, *Acquittal by Resurrection* (New York: Holdt, Rinehart, and Winston, 1964), 16.
2 Regarding Jesus' resurrection as a "prototype for the resurrection of all God's people at the end of the last days," see N. T. Wright, *The Challenge of Jesus: Rediscovering Who Jesus Was and Is* (Downers Grove, IL: InterVarsity, 1999), 145.
3 See the excellent discussion in N. T. Wright, "Jesus' Resurrection and Christian Origins," *Stimulus* 16.1 (Feb 2008): 47–48.
4 Ibid., 42.

Christ has not risen with a *physical* body, then Death and Hades have won, and Jesus' death on the cross was an "epic fail." To neglect the significance of this point is to neglect the portrait of Jesus Christ that Revelation gives us. Jesus cannot claim to be victor over Death and Hades, to "have their keys" (1:18), if, in fact, Death and Hades still have his body! This would be akin to a military dictator claiming to have defeated his enemy while languishing away in the bowels of their dungeon, or for the Los Angeles Rams to claim they were going to win the Super Bowl when, in fact, they were knocked out of the first round of the playoffs.

Thus according to Jesus Christ himself, this "coming back to life" is connected to his conquest of Death and Hades (1:17). Yet it is not just Jesus' own resurrection that Revelation is concerned with. Later, when encouraging those in Smyrna to "be faithful to death" in the midst of persecution (2:10), Jesus prefaces that exhortation with the declaration that he, himself, was once dead but now lives (2:8). In other words, Jesus takes the fear out of death—it is temporary, it has been conquered, and it cannot stop the Christian's witness. In light of the looming resurrection, death itself becomes nothing more than "a rest from their labors" (14:13; cf. 6:11) for martyred Christians.

Furthermore, Revelation tells us of a momentous event that will happen in the future: a "First Resurrection," juxtaposed with "the Second Death." Revelation 20:5–6 seems to indicate that one is either part of one or the other. If one is not a part of the First Resurrection, then that person will have no part in the Second Death, and whether or not one has a part in the First Resurrection depends on whether or not one is united with Jesus, "the Firstborn from the Dead." To be united with the First Resurrected One, Jesus, means participating in the First Resurrection, while not being united with the First Resurrected One means participating in the Second Death. The status of all humanity is inextricably bound up with the status of Jesus Christ. Since he is risen, if we align with him, then we also will be risen. If we align ourselves with the Beast, we face the Second Death, instead.

Where Is Your Allegiance?

Jesus as Ruler of the Nations

Next, Jesus Christ is described as the "ruler of the kingdoms of the earth." This must, once for all, lay to rest the idea of Jesus as *merely* my "BFF."[1] The Jesus of Revelation is a Lamb, true, but he is also a Lion. In Revelation 5:5, the "Lion out of the tribe of Judah" (echoing Genesis 49:8–10) is the one who opens the seals that rains judgment down upon the earth (6:1). The Lion of the tribe of Judah, the rightful king, becomes the instrument of the wrath of God (6:15–17—notice that it is the "kings of the earth," first and foremost, who are terrified of the Lamb; indeed, it is the privileged of the earth who have reason to fear!).

In fact, John here goes to great lengths to demonstrate Jesus' Lordship over *all* the earth, whether they like it or not! In Revelation 1:7, when John quotes a combination of Daniel 7:13 and Zach 12:10–11, he takes Zachariah's specific reference to Jerusalem and expands it to include "every eye" and "all the tribes of the earth." By doing so John accomplishes two things: first, he refutes any anti-Semitic notions that the Jews, specifically, are to be singled out as "Christ-killers" and instead indicates that *everyone* had a hand in "piercing" the Messiah. "Every eye" is guilty, and consequently "every tribe of the earth" (not just the twelve Jewish tribes) will grieve. Secondly, John makes it clear that Jesus will possess ultimate authority not just over Israel, as befitting his Davidic DNA, but over *all* the nations (cf. Revelation 12:5; 15:4; 19:15).

Yet, surprisingly, even as Jesus the Lion comes to *judge* all nations, he also comes to *redeem* all nations. On the one hand, Jesus, as lord of all the kingdoms of the earth, *judges* the kingdoms

---

[1] I appreciate how Peter H. Davids puts it: Although "John has been read as giving us a 'friend in Jesus,' who is our buddy (a misreading of John, but a common one)," in reality "we may be Jesus' people and even his extended family, but we are not his equals. We should say 'sir' when we address him, or, even better, 'your Majesty'" (Davids, *Living in the Light of the Coming King: A Theology of James, Peter, and Jude*, BTNT [Grand Rapids, MI: Zondervan 2014], 301). Davids is speaking specifically of the General Epistles, yet I think the point stands regarding Revelation, as well.

of the earth for participating in the ultimate rebellion of the Beast and the Babylonian Harlot. Yet on the other hand, the end result is *not* the annihilation of the nations (how, then, could Jesus reign over them if they ceased to exist?), but rather his *rescue* of those very nations to heal them.

To be sure, the nations in Revelation are not neutral parties, multiple "Switzerlands"; they are in opposition to the Lamb. In Revelation 13, we see the antichrist, the Beast, seducing the nations—he causes the entire world to look at him in wonder (v. 3), and he subdues "every tribe, people, tongue, and nation" (v. 7). Yet Revelation gives us two views of these nations—on the one hand, they are "duped" by the Beast and by the Harlot (e.g., 13:14). On the other hand, they are the very object of redemption by the Lamb (22:2).

To the extent that the inhabitants of the earth, the nations, orbit their life around the Beast and/or the Harlot, they face the High King's wrath and destruction. So we see, for example, in 17:12–14 a group of "kings" who pledge allegiance to the Beast. The result? The Lamb conquers them, simply on the basis of the fact that the Lamb is "Lord of Lords" and "King of Kings." Likewise, in 20:8–9, the devil deceives the nations with the result that they are destroyed when they oppose the Messiah's Kingdom.

Yet on the other hand, in Revelation 20:3, we see a remarkable event occurring: Lucifer himself is cast into the bottomless pit, *for the express purpose that he will not deceive the nations anymore*, at least for a thousand years. When, after the final rebellion of 20:8–9, the great Deceiver is finally out of the way for good, the Lamb will take and heal the remnant of the nations, thus fulfilling the Davidic prophecy of Psalm 2:10–12. To make sure that the nations are restored to what they should be, the Lamb provides an incredible Garden, a Second Eden, in the grand hub of the earth, the New Jerusalem. This Garden contains the newly restored tree of life, and its leaves sprout for the express purpose of *healing the nations* (Revelation 22:2).

In other words, the return of the true King is not a comprehensive annihilation of all the nations, but a reclamation, a healing, of the nations of the earth! Because the nations are redeemed, healed, Revelation 21:24–27 makes the incredible claim that they can bring their glory, their nobility, their awesomeness, into the New Jerusalem itself (vv. 24, 26)! Not only does the Lamb heal the nations, he makes it so those very nations actually contribute to the glory of the New Jerusalem, something that God Himself created!

Any king needs a nation to rule. The "King of Kings," Jesus Christ, could hardly lay claim to that title if he were to destroy all nations except Israel. Consequently, we see the Lamb ruling *from* the New Jerusalem over the restored nations of the entire earth.[1] Yet far from being the stereotypical conqueror, an Alexander the Great or Genghis Khan, leaving a path of destruction in his wake, the Lamb is a *healing* conqueror. Yes, those who do not submit face his wrath. The Lamb is not a "tame" lion, but a rather violent one. Yet instead of leaving smoldering ruins and apocalypse behind, the Lamb creates a garden to heal those he has subdued. Now this is global domination, Jesus-style!

Christian, have you ever hated a nation? Often times those who have seen the horrors of war firsthand begin to do so. My father, a former missionary to Japan, once met a bitter World War II veteran in America who could not comprehend why anybody would want to offer the love of Jesus Christ to the Japanese. In Japan, many have held bitterness over the atomic bombings of Hiroshima and Nagasaki (not to mention the incredibly more brutal fire bombings of Tokyo). On the other hand, many in Korea and China have understandably harbored anger towards Japan for atrocities during her invasions of Korea and Manchuria. The fact remains: all nations, America, Japan, and the rest of the world, have

---

1   It is worth noting that the Lamb rules as the Jewish, *Davidic* Messiah, thus fulfilling the Abrahamic covenant (for stimulating my thoughts on this regard, I am grateful to Brian Collins, "The Land Promise in Scripture" [paper presented at the Bible Faculty Summit, Watertown, WI, 27 July 2016], 13–14).

been duped by the Serpent, and it is these nations that God wishes to redeem and heal. God's desire to heal these nations does not start with the Great Commission, but rather with the Abrahamic covenant: all the nations of the earth (none of which stand guiltless of atrocity and hatred) will be blessed by the Messiah's healing, at least to some degree. This is *not* contingent on how "good" a nation is or how "nicely" they have historically treated other people. Significantly, in Isaiah 19, after detailing the judgment that will come upon Egypt, the passage makes an incredible statement: the Egyptians will know the Lord, after he has *healed* them (vv. 21–22)! Furthermore, the oracle goes on to say that *Assyria*, of all nations the most violent, brutal, and horrifying, that *Assyria*, together with Egypt and Israel, will be personally blessed by God (23–25)![1]

No nation exists, then, that is beyond the power of God's healing. No matter how brutally it has treated its neighbors (ancient Assyria), no matter how much it has beaten the oppressed slaves within its borders (ancient Egypt and 19th century America), no matter how much land it has stolen without proper compensation (America), no matter how much innocent blood has been shed in aggressive invasion (Japan in World War II), Jesus Christ has come to offer healing.

In the end, however, Jesus reigns only over those who let him heal them. Revelation 21:27 makes it clear that those who, by manner of their unredeemed lifestyle, stand in opposition to him are excluded from the New Jerusalem and the Garden it contains. A doctor does not heal an unwilling patient. Jesus will not force his healing upon those who do not want it. Consequently, we cannot ignore the dichotomy in Revelation between those who allow the "Sun of Righteousness to arise with healing in his wings"[2] and those who raise their fist in hatred and try to blot it out. There will

---

1 I am grateful to my father, John Himes, for reminding me of the theological significance and relevance of the various "nations" being blessed by God in the Old Testament.
2 Paraphrased from what Charles Wesley wrote in his classic hymn "Hark the Herald Angels Sing."

be those who, even as their own nation experiences healing and redemption, find themselves forever without a country, shut out of earth's new capital city.

The Relationship between Jesus and His Followers

We have seen in Revelation 1:5 that Jesus is the Witness, the Resurrected One, and the High King. Yet in each of these three points, Jesus' role is linked to ours: since *he* is a witness, we too become witnesses; since *he* was raised from the dead, we too will be resurrected; since *he* becomes the ruler over all kingdoms, so also we too become a kingdom of priests alongside of him (vv. 5–6).

This idea of us being a "kingdom of priests"[1] is expressed elsewhere in Scripture, and this shows us how we play a key role in the divine cosmic plan God always had for humanity. Adam and Eve were told to "subdue" the earth, i.e., rule over it, not in the stereotypical way we think of "subduing" the earth, which may conjure up images of polluted rivers and strip-mined valleys, but rather as benevolent monarchs, taking care of the earth while guiding and protecting her.[2] Later, in Exodus 19:5–6, the Lord declares to Israel that *if* they obey him, they will become a special treasure for God, a "kingdom of priests" and a "sacred nation" (this is the language echoed in 1 Peter 2:9). Israel's special relation to God was not for the purpose of excluding everybody else, but for the purpose of drawing the other nations to him (Deuteronomy 4:5–8, Psalm 67). The result is a humanity that is finally accomplishing what God intended it to: a benevolent rule over the earth with Jesus Christ as the bearers of the *imago Dei*.[3]

---

1 For this expression, I am following the NIV, which agrees with both the Byzantine (2005) and the Nestle-Aland 27th ed.

2 For an excellent discussion of Adam's role in obeying Genesis 1:28 (and his failure to do so), see G. K. Beale, *A New Testament Biblical Theology* (Grand Rapids, MI: Baker Academic, 2011), esp. 30–37, and 85.

3 See Osborne, *Revelation*, 65, and Beale, *New Testament Biblical Theology*, 62–63.

So we see that everything that is significant about *us* is first and foremost linked to Jesus Christ and who *he* is. *We* are what we are because of *him*! In light of that, we should not be surprised that the rest of the first chapter of Revelation focuses even more on the Son of Man. Beginning with v. 12, we see an almost frightful picture, a picture that causes John himself to fall flat on his face.

ONE LIKE THE SON OF MAN

We are accustomed to benign images of a friendly, smiling Jesus in pop culture, one who does not look as if he were capable of an unkind word. Yet here, in the second half of Revelation 1, John, *who was Jesus' most intimate follower*, cannot help but fall in front of him "as a dead man" (v. 17). Suddenly the Lamb is not so warm and fuzzy anymore. The language used here is loaded with theological significance, and exploring this will demonstrate for us the depths of authority this Figure has, and why the Seven Churches (and we) would do well to listen to him.

First and foremost, this person walking in the midst of seven golden candlesticks is one "like a son of man." This title alludes to what Jesus used to describe himself (e.g., Matthew 8:20; Mark 2:10; Luke 5:24; John 1:51), but this begs the question: what's so special about the title "son of man"? Couldn't basically half the population of the world describe themselves as such? In fact, God himself frequently calls Ezekiel by a similar title (Ezekiel 2:1, etc.). The answer, however, lies in Daniel 7:13–14:

> I saw in the night visions, and, behold, one like the Son of man came with the clouds of heaven, and came to the Ancient of days, and they brought him near before him. And there was given him dominion, and glory, and a kingdom, that all people, nations, and languages, should serve him: his dominion is an everlasting dominion, which shall not pass away, and his kingdom that which shall not be destroyed.[1]

---

1 Quoting from the KJV. The NIV and other versions are very similar.

Where Is Your Allegiance? 23

In fact, one could almost say that Daniel 7:13–14 serves as the "cornerstone" of the entire book of Revelation. Certainly, by the end of the book we see the Father giving over the kingdoms of the world to this cloud-riding "Son of Man" figure, the destruction of all other competing authorities, and the final termination of cosmic conflict.

With Jesus' consistent reference to himself using this terminology, he was essentially saying that *he* is *the* Son of Man that Daniel saw, humanity *par excellence*, especially in such passages as Matthew 24:30, where Jesus describes himself as the "Son of Man coming on the clouds of heaven" (directly parallel to Daniel 7:13). Jesus, then, is not just *any* "son of man," but the one who has ultimate authority over all other "sons of men." In the Daniel passage, this "Son of Man" stands in contrast to the "beasts" in the vision—"That He [Christ] is said to be *like* a son of man, has a significance parallel to that of the prior kingdoms being said to be *like* beasts. Those kingdoms were 'beastly' in character, but His will be 'manly'; that is, humanlike, in all noble proper features."[1] This theological contrast between Jesus and the rulers of the world further develops in Revelation: Jesus as "the Son of Man" stands in opposition to the "Beast[s]" that will appear (e.g., Revelation 13).[2]

In other words, throughout Revelation the reader and listener are confronted with an ongoing conflict, the Son of Man vs. the Beast, a conflict that has its roots in Genesis 3:15. One can follow the Son of Man or one can follow the Beast, but no middle ground

---

1 Leon Wood, *A Commentary on Daniel* (Grand Rapids, MI: Zondervan, 1973), 192.
2 As Thielman notes, after a comparison of Revelation 7:9 and 5:10 with 13:13–14, "John intends by all this a straightforward message. The two beasts and the dragon on one side and God and the Lamb on the other side make the same, totalistic claims. No one, therefore, can legitimately worship both at the same time" (Frank Thielman, *Theology of the New Testament* [Grand Rapids, MI: Zondervan, 2005], 638). Also, note that the godly creatures of chs. 5–6, often translated "beasts," are designated with a different Greek word than *the* Beast of ch. 13f.

exists. Truly Jesus Christ is the only one who could say, "The one who is not with me is against me" (Luke 11:23).

From Revelation 1:13–17, each of the physical descriptions of the "one like a son of man" serves two purposes: to overwhelm the listener/reader with the awesomeness of this figure (like it did John), and to remind us of some key attributes of God Himself. Indeed, almost every one of the elements of the description of this character allude to an Old Testament passage, and many of the descriptions in this passage seem to parallel Daniel 10:5–6.[1] This passage in Daniel seems to portray the "Son of Man" figure as a distinct entity from the mere angels of the rest of the chapter. As one scholar points out, "At least four holy angels ... appear in this vision, and the 'man dressed in linen' is unquestionably in charge."[2]

To begin with, the long robe and the golden sash (specifically around the chest) refer to the noble rank of Jesus Christ, his "exalted, dignified" status, drawing from the description in Daniel 10:5.[3] Whereas once he lived humbly among men, no place to lay his head, dressed like any other average Galilean, now his full glory is revealed. Nobody would mistake him for a common person, for his very presence demands respect! This, of course, draws our attention to the great Christological tension of the Incarnation: the king became a beggar, but is now dressed as a king again. Royalty become a servant, washes the disciples' feet, but now demands ultimate allegiance. The wrists that once allowed nails to pierce them now wield an iron scepter. The Lamb is also a Lion. Neither aspect of Jesus' character can be diminished. Our "best friend" is also our King—there is a time to kiss him in friendship, but also a time to kiss him in fear and reverence (Psalm 2:12), and for John this is clearly the latter! Yet even in the midst of John's terror, the One who demands his unwavering allegiance also says "do not fear," laying the right hand of friendship on John's shoulder. Then, however, the King follows up with a command: "Write."

---

1 See especially Osborne, *Revelation*, 85–93.
2 Stephen R. Miller, *Daniel*, NAC (Nashville, TN: B&H, 1994), 282.
3 Osborne, *Revelation*, 89.

Where Is Your Allegiance?

As for the other descriptions: the "white head and hair," as white as "wool" and "snow" (essentially the purest white possible in that day and age), stem from Daniel 7:9 and 10:6, though with possible allusions to other OT passages (e.g., Ezekiel 1:7).[1] Interestingly, these elements are not actually a description of the Son of Man in Daniel, but rather of the "Ancient of Days." In other words, as Osborne notes, the Son is described in terms of the Father, thus stressing their unity (remember what we said earlier about how the line between terms used to describe the Father and terms used to describe the Son grows fuzzy?)[2]

The blazing eyes, the bronze feet, and the thunderous voice all come, once again, from Daniel 10:6. This presents a fearful sight, and this very image of the Son also occurs in Revelation 2:18, right before Jesus utilizes some of his harshest language to describe what awaits the "Jezebel" of that church.[3]

In summary, what have we learned about this "Son of Man" figure? First, he is clearly divine, possessing a power and a presence that no mere human could possess. Even Moses, who, at least, had a shining face (Exodus 34:35), pales in significance to this figure. Secondly, he is kingly. Whoever he is, he is destined to rule. As such, he demands allegiance and absolute obedience, even from his friends. Thirdly, he deliberately appears as a terrifying figure. Jesus shows no surprise when John falls on his face. Had he wished, the Son of Man could have appeared as the gentle mentor upon whose chest John reclined, but he does not do so at this point in time.

Consequently, because no one else can appear in such a form as the Son of Man, no one else has the right to demand the same amount of loyalty as the Son of Man, either—no pastor, no teacher, no university president, no church leader (either ordained or lay), *no one* has the right to command allegiance, or even a superlative degree of loyalty, except the Son of Man.

---

1 Ibid., 90–91.
2 Ibid., 90.
3 Ibid., 91.

This has practical ramifications. My parents spent 30+ years of loyal missionary service to Jesus Christ, supported by a number of churches in the U.S. One day, my father received a letter (dated July 23rd, 1990) from a large Baptist church whose head pastor was embroiled in a controversy. The letter stated (this is a direct quote), "Due to the charges that have been leveled against [name of church], [name of college] and [personal pronoun reference to head pastor], we feel it necessary to ask each of our missionaries if they are loyal to our ministry and believe in us." Within the same envelope was a card that each missionary had to sign (or lose financial support), which stated, "I believe in [name of church], [name of school], and the leadership of these institutions. Not only am I not disloyal to [name of church, etc.], but I openly defend them when attacked" (this is a direct quote, with the names omitted).

To his everlasting credit, my father did not sign the card, and for good reason. When words such as "believe in" and "loyal to" are carelessly used in reference to human institutions and human leaders, *without careful qualification*, the result is that "Pastor X" and/or "Church X" have taken over language which belongs only to the Son of Man. Yet, as far as the Son of Man is concerned, *there must be no other competitors*!

In other words, although respect and honor are, to a certain degree, appropriate expressions towards a person in authority, unqualified loyalty is not! The moment that the language used to describe your relationship to a human leader (or institution, or political entity) becomes eerily similar to the language used to describe your relationship to Jesus Christ, idolatry has resulted. No one, absolutely no one, other than Jesus Christ has the right to demand unqualified loyalty or faith.

Now, back to discussing Jesus' physical appearance: why, then, does Jesus appear in such a frightening form? Essentially, to pass judgment (positive and negative) upon the seven churches. The Son of Man wishes to make it clear that when he speaks, the churches should listen. There will be no haggling over the grade handed out, no opportunity for retaking a test, no "180 degree performance evaluation" where the opinions of the Christians are just as important as the opinions of the Judge. This judgment will be one-sided, and the one who dishes out justice will tolerate no back-talk. In fact, as has already been noted, the form of the letters to the seven churches prominently resembles the "prophetic lawsuit" addresses from God to the children of Israel in the prophetic books of the Old Testament. In a sense, then, God is taking the seven churches to court.[1] This does not in of itself mean a negative sentence, but it does mean a solemn one. "Christ investigates his churches and audits them based on their faithfulness to covenantal stipulations," and the reason behind this formal "audit" is stated in Revelation 2:23—so that *all* the churches may know that their Lord and Master Jesus Christ is the one who searches out the innermost depths of the heart, and that he will pay back every Christian according to his or her actions.[2]

So we see that Revelation begins with the unveiling of the Son of Man, the key figure of the ages. Before we can actually *hear* what Jesus has to say, we first must *see* him in all his glory, and tremble in fear. Naturally this first chapter of Revelation is hardly the final word of who Jesus is. As Edith Humphrey points out in her excellent book on the rhetoric power of "vision,"

> The full identification of the hero is left until we have met the great Martyr, the slaughtered Lamb, and understood his intimate relationship with the people of God. It is not until the final and great Christophany of chapter 20 that we will move beyond the intimations of the Voice to hear the articulation of Jesus' 'secret' name, inscribed on the thigh, finally and absolutely announced: 'King of Kings and Lord of Lords. Sound, sight, and inscribed word merge in this climactic and unequivocal revelation.[3]

---

1 Bandy, "Patterns of Prophetic Lawsuits," 178–205.
2 Ibid., 185.
3 Edith M. Humphrey, *And I Turned to See the Voice*, STI (Grand Rapids, MI: Baker Academic, 2007), 180.

We do not yet have the full picture of Jesus. We do, however, have enough to get our heart racing and turn a nervous ear to his message to the churches, determined to see what parts speak to us, personally.

QUESTIONS FOR FURTHER DISCUSSION

1. What are the reasons Jesus appears the way he does to John? In what ways should this be both an encouragement and a warning to us?
2. What are some of the ways in which we can end up giving allegiance to others that is due only to Jesus Christ? (Think broadly: job, family, community, nation, church, etc.).

Christians in the Shadow of Empire

Having grown up in Japan, I can attest to a polite, contemplative, beautiful, peace-loving, and socially-unified society, where traditional family units are held in high regard, education is valued (to the point of near-obsession, sometimes), and freedom of religion, at least legally, exists for all.

Yet despite such freedom, the land is still gripped in the oddly synchronic beliefs of materialism, ancestor worship, Shintoism, and Buddhism. Only approximately 0.6% are evangelical Christian,[1] despite over 150 years of Protestant missions. While a remnant remains, that is all it is—a remnant. Consequently, the outward tranquility of the nation belies an inner stress and turmoil. Japan is to my knowledge the only country to coin a specific word for "death from overwork"—*karōshi*. The suicide rate, as of this decade, remains very high (in the top 20),[2] despite its relatively wealthy status.

The lack of Gospel witness in Japan can be traced partially to the capitulation of self-professing Christians to emperor worship and the idolatry of nationalism during World War II. When faced with the choice "reverence the Emperor and serve Japan above all else, or suffer the consequences," by-and-large Christian institu-

---

1 Statistic taken from "The Joshua Project," n.p. [cited 24 November 2016]. Online: https://joshuaproject.net/global_list/countries.
2 See "Suicide Rates by Country," on the World Atlas website, n.p. [cited 22 October 2016]. Online: http://www.worldatlas.com/articles/countries-with-the-most-suicides-in-the-world.html.

tions chose the former. This sad tale has been detailed by, among others, Richard Terrill Baker in his book *Darkness of the Sun: The Story of Christianity in the Japanese Empire*. Baker writes, for example, that

> On numerous occasions the United Church of Christ in Japan was guilty of handing down direct governmental orders to its local churches. One of these cases had to do with the officially prescribed five-minute ceremony of bowing to the emperor and praying for the war heroes just preceding every Christian service of worship. It was a compulsory ritual, and if for any reason it was ever neglected the pastor was immediately taken by the police for questioning.[1]

Furthermore,

> Another errand which the church ran for the government was the publication of a new 'special wartime hymnal,' … Any such reference to Jesus or God as 'King of Kings' was a Shinto sacrilege, and the Christians gave up their usage of the term. 'Onward, Christian Soldiers,' was dropped in the revised hymnal, and while antifascist Norwegian Christians were singing in fields, streets, cottages, and chapels the stirring affirmations of faith in Luther's 'A Mighty Fortress Is Our God,' Japanese Christians were prohibited its use.[2]

We cannot downplay the courage of the many Japanese Christians who *did* suffer for their faith at the hands of the Imperial Japanese Government (indeed, an American friend of mine married the daughter of a Japanese pastor who suffered for his faith). Chapter 8 of Baker's book is devoted to chronicling the faithful endurance of Japanese Christians who chose to suffer rather than submit. Even during the "five-minute ceremony" of emperor reverence mentioned above, many Japanese Christians deliberately came late to the service in order to miss it.[3]

---

[1] Richard Terrill Baker, *Darkness of the Sun: The Story of Christianity in the Japanese Empire* (New York: Abingdon-Cokesbury, 1947), 31.
[2] Ibid., 31–32.
[3] Ibid., 31.

The point, however, is that much of organized Christianity in Japan compromised the integrity of its faith by exalting the nation and the emperor at least to the level of, and often higher than, Jesus Christ. The church in Japan "found [itself] with two gods," and the only way to break such divided loyalty would have meant suffering; thus, "The church of Japan did not choose martyrdom. It accepted the circumscription put upon it by the warring state."[1]

Granted, we must not downplay the agonizing struggle that many believers endure when faced with the decision to suffer or compromise. Japanese novelist Shusaku Endo's book *Silence* demonstrates just how potentially difficult the choice for martyrdom may be. Furthermore, lest we North Americans become too lofty in our own self-evaluation, by the end of the chapter I will make the suggestion that organized Christianity in America has often made the same compromise that much of Christianity in Japan did, at least to some degree.

As we shall see, the first few chapters of Revelation speak exactly to this issue. Revelation 1 is about the Son of Man who owns our allegiance. Much of Revelation 2–3 is about the need to resist any compromise to that allegiance, especially where the Roman emperor and the local gods are concerned. Just two decades after Revelation was written, in approximately 112 A.D., the local Roman governor of Bithynia and Pontus (provinces of Anatolia), named "Pliny the Younger," sent an inquiry to the Emperor Trajan about how to handle those accused of being Christian. Pliny showed genuine concern about not encouraging baseless slander, especially in light of the vast number of accusations being thrown around, but he also adamantly asserted his intention to punish Christians for, at the very least, their "inflexible obstinacy." In order to determine who truly was a Christian and who was not (in light of anonymous accusations), Pliny had this to say:

> A libel was sent to me, though without an author, containing many names [of persons accused]. These denied that they were Christians now, or ever had been. They called upon the

---

1   Ibid., 15.

gods, and supplicated to your image, which I caused to be brought to me for that purpose, with frankincense and wine; they also cursed Christ; none of which things, it is said, can any of those that are really Christians be compelled to do; so I thought fit to let them go. Others of them that were named in the libel, said they were Christians, but presently denied it again; that indeed they had been Christians, but had ceased to be so, some three years, some many more; and one there was that said he had not been so these twenty years. All these worshipped your image, and the images of our gods; these also cursed Christ.[1]

In other words, one way that Pliny made sure the accused were "normal" was to see if they would worship the image of the emperor. This was viewed by the Roman authorities themselves, not just Christians, as incompatible with being a true follower of Jesus Christ. Significantly, the book of Revelation views the churches as already immersed in a struggle for their loyalty. Colin Hemer writes, "Several technical terms of the imperial worship are closely parallel with expressions used in Revelation in a Christian sense, and some of the most telling evidence comes from some of the cities of Asia."[2]

The roots of this conflict between Jesus and Rome, and the choices confronting the Christians of Asia Minor, go back over a century into the history of the conquest of Asia Minor by the Roman Empire. As we explore this history and its implications for society, we must make one thing clear: the cities of Asia Minor were not "oppressed" as we would think of it, fostering a hatred for Rome that was always simmering below the surface, waiting to erupt in a "declaration of independence." Far from it. Reverence for Rome and her emperors was the *normal* state of affairs. Indeed, the cities of Asia Minor actually *competed* over who could honor the Emperor the most![3]

---

1 Pliny the Younger, *Letters*, 10.96–97. Translated by William Whiston.
2 Colin J. Hemer, *The Letters to the Seven Churches of Asia in Their Local Setting* (Grand Rapids, MI: Eerdmans, 1989), 86–87.
3 See Tacitus, *Annals* 4.55.7 and following.

In other words, Christians of Asia Minor, like the faithful Christians of Japan, were not viewed as the "good guys," courageous heroes who dared to stand up to a tyrannical state. To the contrary, Christians were guilty of "rocking the boat" and threatening the status quo. Christian refusal to reverence the emperor made nobody happy.

Asia Minor, modern Turkey, a.k.a. "Anatolia," has always been torn between two worlds. On the one hand, from the days of Cyrus himself Asia Minor belonged firmly within the Persian empire. On the other hand, Greece had a foothold on the region a thousand years before Christ (remember the legend of Troy?). In fact, the relationship between the Persians and the Greek colonies on the coast of Asia Minor consistently caused tension between the two and eventually led to Persia's downfall. To add to its diversity, Asia Minor experienced a vast Celtic-Gallic migration in the early 3rd century BC that significantly impacted Greece and Asia Minor (especially Galatia).[1] In addition, the original ancient inhabitants, the "Hattians" and their ancient conquerors, the "Hittites," both would have left their trace on Asia Minor centuries later.[2]

In a sense, then, Anatolia reveled in its diversity. Even the major Greek cities showed no "impulse towards political unification."[3] Yet, oddly enough, when Rome imposed its imperial agenda on the landmass, Asia Minor rarely instigated any significant uprising. Although Pontus opposed Rome under the infamous Mithridates Eupator from approximately 110–73 BC, and Mithridates' death did not completely terminate the rebellion, yet nonetheless "this great nationalist movement in Asia Minor was also to be the last."[4]

Instead of bloody conquest, then, quite often Rome was given Anatolian cities on- a silver platter. For example, since Rome had

---

1 Stephen Mitchell, *The Celts and the Impact of Roman Rule*, vol. 1 of *Anatolia: Land, Men, and Gods in Asia Minor* (Oxford: Clarendon, 1993), 13–15.
2 For further discussion, see Seton Lloyd, *Ancient Turkey: A Traveler's History* (Berkley: University of California Press, 1989), 32–36.
3 Ibid., 157.
4 Ibid., 175.

assisted Pergamum in fighting off the Seleucids years before Mithridates' opposition, Pergamum's king (who had no heirs) donated his entire kingdom to Rome.[1] Consequently, Pergamum "became the core of the Roman province of Asia" and subsequently "the slow advance of Roman authority in Anatolia seemed irresistible."[2] Nicodemes, possibly copying Pergamum's king, later handed over Bithynia to the Romans. By the time of Mitrhidates' final defeat at the hands of the great Pompey in 63 BC, the Roman army was in a position to eliminate any last vestige of opposition against their hold on Asia Minor.[3] By 51 BC, such Anatolian cities as Galatia were considered substantial assets for building up Roman armies even for campaigns outside Asia Minor.[4] This does not mean, of course, that there was no bloodshed in Asia Minor (much bloodshed stemmed from Rome's own civil wars). Yet one does not see the sort of unified uprising against Roman rule that would characterize either Europe or Israel. Asia Minor sat complacently under the Roman thumb.

Acceptance, indeed *reverence*, of the *pax Romana* became normal for Anatolian culture, putting up a significant obstacle for the acceptance of Christians into society. The imperial cult traces its roots to the deification of Rome herself as *Theia Romei*—the "Goddess Rome." Duncan Fishwick provides the background for this process:

> By the time the Romans first stepped into the Hellenistic World of the eastern Mediterranean, the custom of paying *isotheoi timai* [divine honor] as an expression of homage and gratitude for services rendered had long been in place. It is hardly surprising, then, to find representatives of Roman power, ... treated in much the same way as Hellenistic rulers

---

1 See Mitchell, *Celts and the Impact of Roman Rule*, 29, and Douglas A. Howard, *The History of Turkey* (Westport, CT: Greenwood, 2001), 29.
2 Howard, *History of Turkey*, 29.
3 Lloyd, *Ancient Turkey*, 184–186.
4 Mitchell, *Celts and the Impact of Roman Rule*, 34.

and accorded altars, temples, sacrifices, priests, and games—especially by the Greek cities of Asia Minor.[1]

As early as 195 BC, the inhabitants of Smyrna could boast of a temple to the goddess Roma, built out of gratitude for Rome's assistance against Antiochus III. Similarly, Rhodes, Delphi, and other sister cities also established the same in the 2nd century: "Thereafter her [the Goddess Roma] worship arose elsewhere in the Greek east as Rome pushed eastwards following the defeat of Antiochus and his Aetolian allies."[2] Surprisingly, Roma does not seem to have been a deity the Romans themselves worshipped, but was created by the Greeks and quickly adopted by those to the East as good relations between Rome and the Anatolian cities became important.[3] For Asia Minor, the abstract goddess "Roma" represented the ideas of "peace" and "stability" that Rome herself brought to those under her.[4]

The cult of the goddess Roma then paved the way for the worship of individual emperors. The more Rome came to dominate, the more cities were likely to honor the flesh-and-blood emperor himself, rather than the abstract concept of "Roma," as deity.[5] It must be stressed here that unlike what we would expect with our freedom-loving, individualistic mindset, these centers of imperial reverence were not forced upon the cities of Asia Minor by a Roman government; they were put up voluntarily by local authorities, with little resistance (and much encouragement) from the general populace.[6]

As early as 191 BC, Titus Quinctius Flamininus, the conqueror of Greece, ironically became "the first Roman to be given

---

1 Duncan Fishwick, *The Imperial Cult in the Latin West*, vol. 1 of *Studies in the Ruler Cult of the Western Provinces of the Roman Empire* (Leiden: E. J. Brill, 1993), 46.
2 Ibid., 48–49.
3 Ibid., 48–50.
4 David A. deSilva, *Seeing Things John's Way: The Rhetoric of the Book of Revelation* (Louisville, KY: Westminster John Knox, 2009), 40.
5 Fishwick, *Imperial Cult in the Latin West*, 50–51.
6 deSilva, *Seeing Things John's Way*, 41.

a permanent cult" by the Greeks. Pompey, the defeater of Mithridates, was declared to be "Savior," "Benefactor," and "Creator/Founder" by the inhabitants of the Greek city of Mytilene as well as honored with his own month of the year.[1] This was only the beginning, as the imperial cult spread to Asia Minor. Both Pergamum and Thyateira, two of our seven cities, show evidence of the imperial cult before the birth of Jesus—the former had "local civic cults of Rome" while the latter had an actual temple. Cappadocia developed the imperial cult very early on from its inclusion into the Roman Empire, by A.D. 20.[2] Ephesus, the first city we will study, in 29 BC "rededicated part of its celebrated temple of Artemis to the deified Julius [Caesar] and Roma."[3]

We must be careful, however, not to think of the Imperial Cult (and the worship of Roma, for that matter) as a "religion" in the same way that we think of religion today. Certainly, on the one hand, the function of the imperial cult was political, with an eye towards the stability of the *pax Romana*—"Humanity expressed its loyalty towards the emperor and the government by means of the imperial cult."[4] Whereas each individual city might have her own patron gods, the imperial cult to a certain degree drew all the cities together: "The cult was a major part of the web of power

---

1 Fishwick, *Imperial Cult in the Latin West*, 46–47.
2 Mitchell, *Celts and the Impact of Roman Rule*, 100–102.
3 deSilva, *Seeing Things John's Way*, 40.
4 Friedrich Schröger, *Gemeinde im 1. Petrusbrief* (Passau: Passavia Universtätslage, 1981), 157 ("Die Menschen bekundeten ihre Loyalität gegenüber dem Kaiser und der Regierung im Herrscherkult"). However, Donald Winslow probably goes a bit too far when he argues that "… the Ruler-Cult was never really a religion; … Its purpose was patently to provide a specific focus for the unity of the Empire, for the loyalty of its citizens, and, it must be added, for the control of subversive groups" ("Religion and the Early Roman Empire," in *The Catacombs and the Colosseum*, eds. Stephen Benko and John J. O'Rourke [Valley Forge, PA: Judson, 1971] 247). As S. R. F. Price has argued, one cannot draw a clear line between politics and religion when it comes to the imperial cult (S. R. F. Price, *Rituals and Power: The Roman Imperial Cult in Asia Minor* [Cambridge: Cambridge University Press, 1984], 18–19).

that formed the fabric of society."[1] Yet on the other hand, for the "average Joe" within the cities, no clear-cut distinction would exist between the Imperial State and religion *per se*.[2] Reinhard Feldmeier puts it best: "The State was interpreted religiously; indeed, *it was a sacred institution*."[3]

Rome herself was fully aware of the political power of religion. The Greek historian Polybius, who personally saw Rome's rise to power, had this to say:

> But the quality in which the Roman commonwealth is most distinctly superior is in my opinion the nature of their religious convictions. I believe that it is the very thing which among other peoples is an object of reproach, I mean superstition, which maintains the cohesion of the Roman State. These matters are clothed in such pomp and introduced to such an extent into their public and private life that nothing could exceed it, a fact which will surprise many. My own opinion at least is that they have adopted this course for the sake of the common people.[4]

The dilemma facing Christians in Asia Minor was two-fold. On the one hand, Asia Minor was a (more-or-less) loyal part of the Roman Empire, and each city (if it valued its relationship with Rome) expressed that loyalty, that reverence, in an appropriate manner—temples, festivals, and sacrifices reverencing either the Goddess *Roma* or the emperor himself. On the other hand, each city had its own patron gods and goddesses, and a productive member of the city was expected to participate in cultic festivals honoring them in every sphere of life. Thus New Testament scholar

---

1 Price, *Rituals and Power*, 248.
2 Ibid., 18–19.
3 Reinhard Feldmeier, "Die Außenseiter als savant-garde Gesellschaftliche Ausgrenzung als Missionarische Chance nach dem 1. Petrusbrief," in *Persuasion and Dissuasion in Early Christian, Ancient Judaism, and Hellenism*, eds. Pieter W. van der Horst, et al. (Leuven: Peeters, 2003), 165 ("Der Staat selbst wird religiös gedeutet, ja *er ist eine sakrale Institution*!" Emphasis Feldmeier's).
4 Polybius, *Histories*, 6.56; trans. W. R. Paton.

Larry Hurtado can speak of the "ubiquitous place of the gods in the Roman era.... there were gods acknowledged in practically any significant social setting."[1]

Consequently, to neglect to honor the gods or the Roman emperor in most of Asia Minor would be the equivalent of failing to root for the Green Bay Packers in eastern Wisconsin: more than unthinkable! Yet that "Packers" analogy falls a bit short, however. If Wisconsinites were anything like the Romans, they would not say, "Cheer for the Packers, not the Vikings." Instead, they would say, "Cheer for whoever you want, Bears, Vikings, it doesn't matter, so long as you pay due respect for the Packers by visiting the shrine (Lambeau Field!) once a year, reverence the quarterback at social functions, and make the appropriate offerings of cheese. Otherwise you hate your city, you hate your country, and if any famine or flooding harms our crops, it's all because you failed to pay homage to the Packers!"

In other words, religion in the Roman world was very pluralistic, to a certain degree: "Worship whomever you want, so long as you reverence the local gods and Caesar." To neglect to do so is to turn one's back on country and kin. Worse, to neglect to honor the gods is to be an "atheist."[2] As we shall see, Christian exclusive reverence of Jesus Christ would cause problems and friction with neighbors in many, if not all, of the cities addressed in Revelation 2–3. Indeed, the concept of *exclusive* allegiance to a particular god at the exclusion of all others, especially those of your own nationality, was a bizarre concept for Greco-Roman society as a whole![3]

---

1 Larry W. Hurtado, "The Distinctiveness of Early Christianity," *Catalyst*, n.p. [cited 25 November 2016]. Online: http://www.catalystresources.org/the-distinctiveness-of-early-christianity/.
2 Hurtado, "Distinctiveness of Early Christianity," n.p.
3 See the helpful discussion in Larry W. Hurtado, *Destroyer of the Gods: Early Christian Distinctiveness in the Roman World* (Waco, TX: Baylor University Press, 2016), 29–31, 91–94, etc. Indeed, Christianity was definitely considered different and even weird to society around them. Hurtado states, "In this [a religious exclusivism that was trans-ethnic], I submit, we have a new kind of religious identity that is very different from what

The modern North American or European may struggle understanding such a degree of "group conformity" in our heavily individualized society. Yet the ancient near east (and much of the far east) for the most part consisted of what is called an "Honor and Shame" society, especially at the group level. In other words, how one acted and how one fulfilled his or her obligations towards a social unit (family, town, club, local gods, emperor, etc.) either confirmed or threatened the honor of the social unit itself.[1] In many nations under Rome, including Asia Minor, "Participating in the cults of Rome, the emperor and the traditional pantheon showed one's *pietas* or εὐσεβεία, one's reliability, in effect, to fulfill one's obligations to family, patron, city, province and empire.... Imperial cult in all parts of the empire focused attention on the emperor as the patron of the world."[2] This is vividly illustrated by a papyri letter in the British Museum, dated to approximately 194 AD, where the emperor Tiberius acknowledges receipt of a gift from the "Gymnastic Club of Nomads"; in his response the Caesar states this this was "an expression of your loyal devotion [*eusebeias*, a term frequently used in religious contexts] towards me."[3]

Consequently, anybody who refused to reverence the emperor along with the rest of his town, club, or whatever, was "not a team player," and did not care about the well-being of others. "By withdrawing from cultic expressions of solidarity with the citizenry and

---

was typical of the Roman period" (*Destroyer of the Gods*, 89). Another way in which the God of Judaism and Christianity was "weird" to the Greco-Roman world was the idea that God could "love" humans and expect "love" in response. For an excellent discussion, see Hurtado, *Destroyer of the Gods*, 62–66.

1 For a fascinating discussion of the relationship between "honor and shame" and the imperial cult, see the essay by Richard Warren Johnson, "Confronting the Beast: The Imperial Cult and the Book of Revelation," in *Essays on Revelation: Appropriating Yesterday's Apocalypse in Today's World*, ed. Gerald L. Stevens (Eugene, OR: Pickwick, 2010), esp. 131–132.
2 David A. deSilva, "Honor Discourse and the Rhetorical Strategy of the Apocalypse of John," *JSNT* 71 (1998): 3.
3 "Extracts from a Diploma of Club Membership" (Papyri Brit. Mus. 1178; c. AD 194). Trans. George Milligan.

loyalty and gratitude toward those who secured the well-being of the city, Gentile Christians especially were held in suspicion and stood at risk of being viewed as subversive, unreliable and even dangerous elements of society."[1]

At the heart of the matter is the issue of *allegiance* and *reverence*, two concepts which go hand in hand. To whom does the Christian owe allegiance? Who or what can receive reverence? We are not speaking of *respect* or *honor*, a completely different concept. In fact, elsewhere in the New Testament, the Apostle Peter commanded Christians in Asia Minor to *honor* the Roman emperor, but to honor him *as just another man*, not a demi-god.[2] I believe John would have agreed—it is one thing to honor and respect the emperor (and all other human beings, as Peter made clear), but it is another thing altogether to reverence or to pledge allegiance to somebody. We do not need to see any theological contradiction between Peter, Paul, and John, as if the first two were "pro-emperor" and John was "anti-emperor."

What, then, is the difference between allegiance and reverence on the one hand, and respect and honor on the other? Namely, the *amount* and *quality* of positive attention given somebody determines whether or not you are reverencing them instead of respecting them. This, I believe, is a key point of 1 Peter 2:13–17— the minute one starts to reverence the emperor (or any leader) *as anything other than a man or woman put in a specific position*, then this has crossed the line from "honor and respect" to "reverence and worship."

Thus for a Christian in Asia Minor to honor the emperor means to obey his laws (that do not conflict with God's), to pray for his well-being, and not to disrespect him (mocking, insult,

---

1 deSilva, "Honor Discourse," 84.
2 For the idea that 1 Peter's admonition in 2:13 is actually countering the claims of the imperial cult, I am indebted to an article by Travis B. Williams, "The Divinity and Humanity of Caesar in 1Peter 2, 13," *ZNW* 105 (2014): 131–147. As Williams points out, the language of 2:13 deliberately and blatantly stresses that the emperor was *a created being* (see esp. 133–135, 143–144).

etc.). To *reverence* the emperor, however, means to offer a sacrifice before his image (essentially saying he is greater than any man), to acknowledge his title as "Savior of the World," and even to attend a meal where the meal itself makes clear that the emperor is above all other men. This very issue matters for the study of Revelation, for in Revelation "John repeatedly insists that the failure to reserve divine honors exclusively for God and the Lamb, while it may result in temporary advantage, is ultimately the path to greater disadvantage."[1]

This is the very issue that still confronts believers today: *who deserves reverence?* The answer to this question can affect the lifestyle of every Christian. Japan, for example, has much *legal* religious freedom, perhaps even more so than America, yet pressure from society and family can be nearly unbearable for Japanese Christians. My parents, having been missionaries to the Japanese for 30+ years, have known of cases where becoming a Christian was no big deal so long as one still reverenced and prayed to one's ancestors, but either repudiating ancestor worship or getting publicly baptized would result in being disowned. For the former, by ceasing to worship one's ancestor one ceases to be Japanese (in the minds of many). For the latter, baptism meant exclusive identification with Christ over all other entities (dead ancestors, the Emperor, the nation of Japan itself, etc.).

Similarly, I once heard a missionary to Thailand discuss how, in certain cases, for a member of the family to convert from Buddhism to Christianity meant (in the eyes of society and family) that they did not care about their family any more, that they essentially despised their parents. In such cases, simply by virtue of becoming a Christian, a Thai believer "dishonored" his or her family and was consequently shunned by them. The Thai believer had to make a difficult choice: *as a loyal subject of Jesus Christ, what degree of honor am I allowed to give others?* A line exists that cannot be crossed.

Sadly, I can think of an illustration from my own independent Baptist circles (broadly speaking) where honor has been replaced by

---

1   deSilva, "Honor Discourse," 89.

reverence. There are at least two immensely influential independent Baptist leaders of the 20th century who, after they died, received statues made of them. Considering the fact that *God himself* does not allow statues to be made of himself or anything else (Exod 20:4), it is worth asking: has this gone too far? Are they being honored in such a way that puts them above other men and women (and, one could argue, above God himself?) My personal conviction is that the answer is "yes."

One of those who posthumously received a statute in his honor was also the one, mentioned in an earlier chapter, whose received various statements of loyalty from missionaries the church financially supported. Obviously, we must acknowledge that certain people (e.g., one's spouse) require a certain degree of loyalty. The problem, however, is that this call for "not being disloyal" included also a demand for *unequivocal* defense of this particular pastor (and other church leaders), when in reality only Jesus can demand *unequivocal* defense; only Jesus can say, "If you oppose me, you're in the wrong." All other humans who have ever lived cannot and must not assume that others take their word on faith. Only Jesus holds the right to be taken strictly on faith, with no possibility that he might be wrong.

In the case of the example mentioned above, a few (fortunately only a few!) missionaries began wearing badges stating they were "100% for" this particular pastor. Consider what this means: if I am "100% for a particular football team," then I will never, ever, oppose them (else I would not truly be "100% for" them!). No matter what the circumstances, no matter who they are playing, no matter if the entire team showed up drunk and the coach joined ISIS, I would still not oppose them if I am truly "100% for" them. Otherwise the phrase "100% for" loses meaning if there is any qualification.

To say, then, that one is "100% for" somebody has crossed the line from honor to reverence because it has placed that person above all other men and women on earth. To be "100% for" a particular person, whether it be the Emperor, the President, or a

Where Is Your Allegiance? 43

Baptist preacher, means that such a person becomes an object of faith, with no possibility of critical evaluation. Yet only one Person who ever existed should be an object of faith: namely, Jesus Christ. If I am "100% for" any person other than Jesus Christ, then that person has become the equal of Jesus Christ, and I am incapable of siding with Jesus Christ against that other person. Worse yet, if that other person has sinned, and I am 100% for that person, then now I am in the unenviable position of siding with that other person *against* Jesus Christ (significantly, not even King David encouraged his subjects to be "100% for" him; otherwise, how could Nathan have confronted him over sin?).

Now, at this point I will enter into some even more controversial application. Remember, from our study earlier, that emperor reverence had its roots in *empire* reverence, in the form of an oddly abstract goddess named *Roma*. In other words, imperial nationalism (especially from non-Italians, ironically) morphed into reverence and worship. This has been the case with many societies throughout history.

Yet it's quite possible the same danger has confronted Americans, and carelessly slipped through the door we left open.

Consider the following: in September 1892, in the magazine *The Youth's Companion*, the Baptist socialist Francis Bellamy published his *Companion Address* to the new Pledge of Allegiance. Within this address (the full text is available to anybody—see the citation), Bellamy made a number of interesting statements including his declaration that the public school system was "the noblest expression of the principle of enlightenment which Columbus grasped by faith," that Columbus' achievement represented a "new social order, the celebration of liberty and enlightenment organized into a civilization." Bellamy's desire was to "exalt the free school that embodies the American principle of universal enlightenment and equality: the most characteristic product of the four centuries of American Life." Furthermore, "True Americanism," for Bellamy, was "the leadership of manhood; equal rights for every soul; universal enlightenment as the source of progress." Even more significantly, Bellamy stated, "Faith in the underlying principles of Americanism and in God's destiny for the Republic makes a firm ground of hope."[1]

Ignoring for a second the other problematic statements, let's focus on that last sentence: "Faith in the underlying principles of Americanism and in God's destiny for the Republic makes a firm ground of hope." The problem is that: (1) "Americanism" has suddenly become equal with "God's destiny", and (2) "faith in Americanism" becomes the basis of "hope." Both of these statements are manifestations of the worst form of pagan syncretism, the fusing of pagan ideals (the goddess *Roma*—in this case the goddess "Lady Liberty," a.k.a. "True Americanism") with the worship of the one true God.

Christians must consistently live in such a way that there can be no doubt where their allegiance lies: Jesus Christ first, then family and country as an infinitely distant 2nd and 3rd place. No blurring of the lines can be tolerated. Christians who give the impression that "Americanism" walks hand in hand with "Christianity" have failed in their witness by confusing the sacred with the secular. Richard T. Baker, when bemoaning the failure of much of organized Christianity in Japan during World War II, aptly states,

> When a religion accommodates itself to the social milieu in which it moves, it becomes chameleon-like and indistinguishable from the environment which surrounds it. This was the way in which Christianity in wartime Japan sacrificed its message and lost its uniqueness and evangelizing power. The sharpest criticisms I heard of Christianity in Japan did not come from foreigners but from sensitive Japanese themselves who said that wartime Christianity failed in Japan

---

[1] The text is taken from http://undergod.procon.org/view.additional-resource.php?resourceID=78 [cited 7/30/2015], n.p. For a physical copy, the reader may consult pages 662–663 of Edward Mark Deems (ed.), *Holy-Days and Holidays: A Treasury of Historical Material in Full and Brief, Suggestive Thoughts, and Poetry, Relating to Holy Days and Holidays* (New York: Funk and Wagnall's, 1902).

because it offered the people nothing more than they could get from the government's propaganda.¹

Yet let's bring this closer to home. When within corporate worship, the very place where *the divine Father and the Lamb* are supposed to be exalted *above all others*, we sing songs of praise to our country or even specific branches of military service (however valorous they may have been), does not the setting itself mean that we have crossed the line from *honor* to *reverence*? In other words, would not an unbeliever, sitting within a church congregation, suddenly cease to see a difference between what is offered in church and what is offered at a local July 4th parade? The point is not that the music at a July 4th parade is necessarily "worldly"; rather, the point is that *it has no place side-by-side with music honoring God in corporate worship*. Indeed, it is quite counterproductive. I think especially of "The Air Force Song" which in the first verse specifically encourages the use of guns against the nation's enemies; while this is understandable in a patriotic parade (setting aside for the moment issues of Christian ethics), how can this be sung in corporate worship by the same lips who, just last week, sang "For God so Loved the World"? Could not such incredible irony harm the church's message?

There is an appropriate place to honor one's country and, some may argue, those who selflessly serve to protect the homeland. That place, however, is not corporate worship of the one true God. To place America side-by-side with the Lord of the universe denigrates the latter and exalts the former. If we have the audacity to do so, we must not be surprised when the latter treats the former like Dagon in 1 Samuel 15.

At its best, patriotic expressions in corporate worship blur the line between patriotism and reverence, opening the door to the very religious syncretism that, as we shall see, threatened some of the churches of Asia Minor. At its worst, extreme nationalism has become idolatry. As David Alan Black states, "There is perhaps no clearer example of the church's misguided appropriation of the

---
1 Baker, *Darkness of the Sun*, 69.

world than the god of nationalism."[1] That which receives songs of praise on an equal level with the Father and the Lamb (even if it's only a couple times a year), that which is exalted to heavenly heights as the object of loyalty—such an object, whether human being or political entity, has become an idol.

I wish to make clear that I am not criticizing *patriotism* or any expression of "honor." This is appropriate—God himself blesses the "nations," and seems to assume that each nation will hold a special place in the heart of her inhabitants. Precisely because it is natural for one to belong to a nation, the Bible tells us to treat the "foreigner," the displaced person, with love and compassion (e.g., Exodus 22:21—how different this is from many evangelicals' attitude towards immigrants!) Affection and honor for one's nation is important, so long as love is maintained for the outsider.

What I believe the Bible opposes is "exceptionalism," namely the concept that one's nation is greater than all others and worthy of *special* honor. In the eyes of God, all nations are as a "drop in the bucket" (Isaiah 40:15). Furthermore, as we saw in ch. 1, the "nations" in Revelation initially stand in opposition to the Lamb and must be rescued before they are fit to walk in the new Jerusalem. Yet even when they are redeemed, there is no "special status" for America, Japan, or any other modern political entity. They all orbit around the great capital city, the New Jerusalem. The problem is that many of us have treated *our* particular nation as if it has a special status, a special covenant under God (how often have I heard 2 Chronicles 7:14 quoted during a July 4th sermon in reference to the USA!). Yes, our country of residence should have a certain degree of our loyalty (even if we are living in a foreign country—see Jeremiah 29:7), but it must not claim our reverence.

Furthermore, *a nation already exists which must claim our first loyalty*, namely the kingdom of Jesus Christ (1 Peter 2:10). Indeed, the geographical and political entity known as the United States of America, like all other "nations" in Revelation, *can* and *will* come into conflict with the Kingdom of God, manifested via the

---

1 David Alan Black, *Christian Archy* (Gonzalez, FL: Energion, 2009), 1.

Church (both local and universal). So long as there exists any area where Jesus Christ is not King in men's hearts, there is opposition to the Kingdom of God. Appeals to "Christian democratic ideals" (whatever those might be) or "the faith of our founding fathers" (which has been overstated—reference to a deity or public prayer does not make one a Christian) are all irrelevant—no person or political entity which does not confess Jesus Christ as King and does not live as if it were the case has any right to claim to be "part of a Christian nation."

Here, then, are the points I am trying to make. First, Revelation makes it very clear that, of all humans who ever lived, only Jesus Christ deserves our reverence and "100% loyalty." No emperor, king, president, pop star, athlete, pastor, or preacher must even begin to approach the level of affection and respect we offer Jesus Christ.[1] Second, as we shall see, the churches in Revelation are constantly reminded that their primary loyalty lies with the Kingdom of Heaven, and that the corrupt world systems stand in opposition to it (and them). The churches of Revelation primarily face the temptations of synchronism and compromise, allowing the attitudes of the world (including emperor worship and reverence for the Roman empire, as well as her gods) to affect their own life. To these seven churches, however, Jesus Christ appears with flaming eyes and blinding white hair to announce that *he alone* demands their allegiance.

QUESTIONS FOR FURTHER DISCUSSION

1. What is the difference between appropriate respect given to one's nation, and crossing the line into religious "reverence"?

---

[1] I appreciate the following statement by Johnson, "Confronting the Beast," 143: "As portrayed by John the characteristics of the Beast are (a) demand for allegiance that belongs only to God, and (b) the exploitation of the weak for the benefit of the powerful. When such conditions prevail, John's call to the church is 'Come out!'"

2. In what ways might an "imperial cult" develop even in today's society, and how might this result in the persecution of Christians?

EPHESUS — LOSING YOUR FIRST LOVE

THE BACKGROUND OF EPHESUS

As the Apostle John's letter carrier trudged down the dusty Roman road towards Ephesus, he may have either been intimidated, eager, or both. Ephesus was the city where exciting things happened, a modern day New York, the "most cosmopolitan" of the seven cities,[1] a hodgepodge of public baths, gymnasiums, plenty of magnificent temples, and even a gladiator arena, teeming with a population of over 200,000.[2] Though initially opposed to Roman rule (assisting Mithridates in his uprising), nevertheless Ephesus benefited greatly from the *pax Romana*, becoming a great harbor and bastion of trade (thanks to its location by the Cayster River and the Aegean Sea), developing into the third most important city in the entire Roman empire behind Rome and Athens.[3]

According to Strabo, the ancient city was first inhabited by the mythical Amazonians, who were in turn driven out by the Ionians. The Ionians, however, in their quest to build a superior civilization, kept and amplified one feature of the old city: the temple of "the

---

1 Hemer, *Letters to the Seven Churches of Asia*, 35.
2 Harold W. Hoehner, *Ephesians: An Exegetical Commentary* (Grand Rapids, MI: Baker Academic, 2002), 83, 88.
3 Hemer, *Letters to the Seven Churches of Asia*, 35–36, and Hoehner, *Ephesians*, 87–88.

great Anatolian mother-goddess," whom they worshipped under the name of their own Artemis.[1]

In the mid-500s, Croesus of Lydia conquered Ephesus but took good care of Artemis' (a.k.a. Diana's) temple. Though the temple was burned down by an insane man named Herostratus, its replacement soon become one of the "Seven Wonders of the World," renowned throughout the empire as a building truly worth worshipping at! The passion with which the Ephesians regarded the cult and temple of Artemis/Diana can be seen in Acts 19, where simply the threat of dishonor to Artemis (and the silversmiths' livelihood) started a riot.

Besides its incredible grandiose presentation, Artemis' temple further transcended the mundane shrines of other "lesser" cities in other ways. First of all, this temple had a reputation for being used as a "criminal" sanctuary, a "place of refuge" that offered "salvation" (the same word *sōtēria* that is used in the New Testament). Not surprisingly, the sanctuary often functioned as a den of criminal activity, to the despair of the city's inhabitants.[2] In addition, two other fascinating features marked Artemis' temple: her "paradise" garden and the myth of the "goddess tree"; the significance of these will be discussed below.[3]

Diana/Artemis was hardly the only entity worshipped in Ephesus, of course, In addition to the normal motley assembly of deities, Caesar Augustus was honored with two different temples in the city while Domitian himself declared Ephesus to be "the guardian of the imperial cult."[4] This most likely put enormous pressure on the believer's church, since Domitian "enforced his worship with a rigor hitherto unknown."[5]

The Ephesian church, then, is surrounded by deities, human and mythological, all clamoring for their attention. These gods,

---

1   Hoehner, *Ephesians*, 81.
2   Hemer, *Letters to the Seven Churches of Asia*, 48–49.
3   Ibid., 45–47, 50–51.
4   Witherington, *Revelation*, 95.
5   Hemer, *Letters to the Seven Churches of Asia*, 40.

goddesses, and demi-gods are not in competition, for they are quite happy to exist together and share the mortals' worship. Yet their call for reverence stands in opposition to the One who confronts these believers; the good news is that the Ephesian believers have actually performed quite well in resisting the cacophony of calls to worship. The bad news is that they lost something vital in the process.

Jesus' Message to Ephesus

"So says the one ...."—these opening words of the Lamb, both here and in the other six letters, deliberately call to mind the Old Testament prophetic utterances: "Thus saith the Lord."[1] This is not a casual "What's up?" or "How's it going," but a formal utterance for a serious matter. In fact, the description of Jesus in Revelation 2:1 is meant to be somewhat intimidating: instead of simply "holding" the seven stars in his hand, as in previous verses (1:16, cf. 1:20), here John uses a different Greek word than in 1:16—now he is "grasping" the seven stars.[2] Whoever these "angels" are that the stars represent,[3] Jesus fully possesses them. Furthermore, the fact that Jesus walks among the seven candlesticks (i.e., the churches) demonstrates his sovereign authority over them, especially given his threat in 2:5 to remove this particular candlestick from its place. The Lamb is not one to be trifled with; he is not one who can be put on hold. His word is sovereign, and Ephesus would do well to

---

1 See Thomas B. Slater, *Christ and Community: A Socio-Historical Study of the Christology of Revelation* (Sheffield, England: Sheffield Academic, 1999), 113, and Osborne, *Revelation*, 111. This fact, of course, nicely supports Bandy's point regarding the "prophetic lawsuit motif" noted earlier (Bandy, "Patterns of Prophetic Lawsuits").

2 Osborne, *Revelation*, 112.

3 Scholarship is divided on this topic. The most popular theories seem to be: 1. Specific supernatural angels assigned to each church; 2. The pastor/bishop of each church; and 3. The literal "messenger" (one of the meanings of the Greek word *angelos*) for each church. For the best treatment of this topic, as well as his own unique view that the "*angelos*" for each church is the one actually reading the letter to each church, see Everett Ferguson, "Angels of the Churches in Revelation 1–3: *Status Quaestionis* and Another Proposal," *BBR* 21.3 (2011): 371–386.

remember that. Indeed, it is quite possible that Ephesus, given her position as the "mother church of the region," especially needed to be reminded of this fact: "Since Ephesus is the mother church, she must realize that Christ, not her, 'holds the seven stars' and 'walks among the lampstands.' There is no room for pride, for it is Christ alone who is sovereign, not any church."[1]

I believe this point is worth expanding. If, in fact, as great a church as Ephesus was *not* indispensable to the work of God in Asia Minor, what does that say about many local churches today? Size obviously does not guarantee one's continued usefulness before God (as Ephesus found out), and, to our surprise, neither does fidelity to orthodoxy. In other words, today even the largest and most theologically orthodox of churches must stop and evaluate herself—neither "look how big we are" nor "look how theologically correct we are," *in of themselves*, can stop the Lamb from plucking out one's place among his churches. Ephesus, like many churches today, was lacking a key ingredient, and this is what put them in danger *in spite of* their correct doctrine.

Yet before we get to this negative criticism of Ephesus, let us examine how the Lamb praises them. First of all, he notes their "work, labor, and patience," specifically in opposition to apostates. Indeed, the Ephesus church is to be commended for "testing" those claiming to be apostles (cf. 1 John 4:1, though different terminology is used), and finding out that they are liars.

We must stress, however, that this "testing" the claims of so-called apostles must have involved looking at both their doctrine *and* their lifestyle. In John's first epistle (ch. 4), as well as apostolic literature such as Galatians, 2 Peter 3, etc., analysis of one's theology is essential. Paul feels so strongly about the core doctrine of the Gospel, for example, that in Galatians he curses anybody who would distort it, even if it were an angelic being (and this is not a casual "may all your vacation pictures be lost when your hard drive crashes" type of curse either; Paul desires, rather, the eternal condemnation of those who unrepentantly mess with the Gospel).

---
1 Osborne, *Revelation*, 111.

Interestingly, however, in 2 Peter 2 and Jude, the immoral lifestyle of the heretics is emphasized more than their doctrine (and James speaks dogmatically of the emptiness of orthodoxy without good works; James 2). Chapters 2–3 of Revelation routinely condemn *both* false doctrine and immoral lifestyle, as we shall see. Thus to "test" those calling themselves apostles (or preachers, or evangelists, or Bible teachers) involves an examination of both their belief system and their lifestyle (within appropriate measure, of course; John is not calling us to be stalkers or busybodies).

I believe this is made clear in v. 6—"you hate *the deeds* of the Nicolaitans, whom I also hate." On the one hand, the "Nicolaitans" are a specific group of people marked out by an ideology. Interestingly, the noun derives from the Greek word *"nikaō,"* and so Ben Witherington appropriately labels this group as the so-called "Victory People" (I will continue to borrow Witherington's term in this chapter).[1] On the other hand, the beliefs of the "Victory People" are revealed in *their deeds*, i.e., what they do is based on what they believe. Consequently, the two go hand-in-hand. We must not say, on the one hand, "It doesn't matter what you believe so long as you act right," yet neither can we say "He may be a jerk but at least he believes what I believe!" (which, come to think of it, is quite often the justification for how people vote in politics).

We see, then, this theme repeated throughout Revelation. In Jesus' message to Pergamum, the "teaching" of Balaam is linked to both eating food offered to idols and sexual sin. The so-called "Jezebel," in the church at Thyatira, both "teaches" and "seduces" to immorality (immorality naturally follows from bad teaching). On the one hand, in order to be accepted into the Kingdom, one must accept Jesus Christ for who he is and reject the Beast and his false claims—i.e., doctrine. Jesus "witnesses" to the churches about himself (22:16), and those who fail to accept that "witness" are condemned. Yet on the other hand, when we reach the final warning of Revelation (22:8), the basis for exclusion from the kingdom is

---

1 Witherington, *Revelation*, 96.

immorality and other sins that have not been atoned for (cf. 1:5). In other words, lifestyle cannot be dislocated from doctrine.

So the Ephesians, at the very least, effectively analyzed those claiming to bear the truth on the basis of both their ideology *and* their lifestyle. For this they were worthy of praise.

The problem, however, is that they lost their "first love" (or "primary love"), a somewhat ambiguous statement that, although no doubt clear to the original audience,[1] leaves us scratching our heads. How do you lose your "first love" and how do you get it back (all without sounding like a cheesy country song)? The key, I believe, is to focus on the connection between the problem ("you have lost your first love") and the solution ("do the first/primary works") of 2:5.

The Apostle John, of course, is well-known for his focus on love in all of his writings. In fact, of the two main Greek verbs for "love" in the Bible (*agapaō* and *phileō*), John's writings account for just over *half* the total occurrences of those two verbs. Clearly, then, "love" plays a major role in John's work. More significantly, when we focus on Jesus' words in John 14, we see this same link between "loving" and "doing" that we find in Revelation 2:4–5. Jesus tells his disciples that if they truly love him, they will obey his words (John 14:15, 21, 23–24). Consequently, love means action. In order to truly claim to love Jesus more than anything else, one must obey what Jesus says.

This, of course, would broadly include all Jesus has to say about the Spirit-filled life (and notice how the Spirit is linked to loving and obeying Jesus in John 14:15–31). However, I believe we can get a bit more specific. When Jesus asks Peter if he loves him in John 21:15–17, Jesus repeatedly tells Peter to take care of "my lambs/sheep," i.e., the flock of God around him. Furthermore, back in John 13:34–35, Jesus declares that the mark of discipleship is that Peter and the others love each other. In fact, John repeats Jesus' message and expands on it in his first epistle, 1 John 2:3–11

---

1 As pointed out in Slater, *Christ and Community*, 117.

Where Is Your Allegiance?

(notice also 4:7–11). In other words, *loving each other is the sign that we love Jesus* (cf. Matthew 22:39)!

Here's the theological flow of thought then: (a.) Jesus is our primary love;[1] (b.) Jesus said, "If you love me, obey me"; (c.) One of Jesus' main imperatives in the Johannine literature is "love one another"; (d.) Consequently, it makes sense that the Ephesians must get back to this key aspect of Jesus' teaching, namely, loving one another, if they truly wish to claim they love him.[2]

The solution for Ephesus, then, has three parts: remember, repent, and perform. The idea of "remembering" is absolutely essential to repenting, and we see this quite a bit in the Old Testament. God's people are called to "remember" in order to "repent" (cf. Isaiah 44:21).[3] Indeed, it is impossible to change our lifestyle, our habits, if we do not take time to direct our mind to God's standard. Once the right path is before us, only then can we commit ourselves to a new path, i.e., "repent." This is like a driver who suddenly realizes she took the wrong exit. This person must first visualize where she went wrong and what the right exit was ("remember"), then commit herself to a new course of action ("repent"), and then alter her route appropriately ("do"). Attempting the third step without the first two steps will result in a shallow and legalistic attitude. On the other hand, the first two steps are worthless without the third step.

The Ephesians, then, must recall their initial attitude of love they had towards Jesus and towards each other, an attitude that manifested itself in concrete action: caring for each other, not sinning against each other, encouraging each other (and rebuking,

---

1 Interestingly, in Josephus, *Antiquities* 18.64 (possibly a Christian interpolation since they were, after all, the ones preserving the works of Josephus), in reference to the crucifixion, states, "Those that loved him at the first [very similar language to what Jesus says to the church in Ephesus] did not forsake him, for he appeared to them alive the third day" (trans. William Whiston).
2 See cite Witherington, *Revelation*, 96, for a similar conclusion, though the train of thought is my own.
3 Osborne, *Revelation*, 116–117.

when necessary), making sure one's brothers and sisters have the basic necessities of life, etc. They must perform "the 'acts of love' toward God and one another that characterized the early years of their church."[1] Otherwise, their very existence as a church is in danger.[2] In other words, Jesus seems to be declaring that a lousy, loveless attitude in a church is just as quick a way for its destruction as lousy, heretical theology.

Interestingly, though, Jesus closes his admonition by once again praising them for opposing heretics, the so-called "Victory People." It's as if, having rebuked them sharply on their lovelessness towards *people*, Jesus nevertheless did not want them to lose their hatred towards heresy. In other words, the truly mature church must have *both* a hatred for heresy *and* a love for the unlovable!

This, of course, begs the question: what is heresy? Here we must be extremely careful, for two ditches straddle the theological road each church is on. First, on the right side is the tendency for some churches (and preachers) to magnify relatively minor matters to issues of contention (sometimes not just contention, but all-out thermonuclear warfare!). Sadly, specific Bible versions (usually the King James), one's view of the end times, the role of "deacons" and "pastors," etc. have occasionally been elevated to the level of the Gospel itself. I once heard a sermon where a particular view of the "rapture" was labeled a "false Gospel." This would have astonished the apostle Paul, whose definition of the Gospel in 1 Corinthians 15 involves the atoning death, burial, resurrection, and eyewitness testimony of the Messiah (all according to the Scriptures), and absolutely nothing about particular views on the "rapture."

On the other side of the road, however, is a different type of ditch, one marked by the conclusion that all beliefs are "ok" so long as one "loves." Yet by using this extremely strong term, "hate" (not "frown at," or "disapprove," or "ignore"), Jesus gives us no leeway. We can love and tolerate *people* (while attempting to draw them

---

1 Ibid., 117.
2 See Osborne, *Revelation*, 118, for support of the idea that this represents "apostasy and the subsequent loss of their status as a church."

to the truth), but any belief system that opposes the undisputed, core truths about Jesus Christ must be vehemently opposed. Certain points of doctrine cannot disappear without radically altering Christianity to the point where it ceases to be Christianity.

What, then, are the core doctrines worth fighting for without quarter, whose denial threatens the very foundation of Christianity? That is a question that cannot be fully answered here, despite its relevance for our theology of Revelation 2. For a good starting point, I would direct the reader to Craig L. Blomberg's article, "The New Testament Definition of Heresy (Or When Do Jesus and the Apostles Really Get Mad?)"[1] as well as Osborne's excellent discussion on the essentials of the faith in his commentary on this passage.[2] Personally, I would especially stress the content of the Gospel (Jesus Christ's death for our sins and literal resurrection, all according to Scripture and all verified via his burial and eyewitness accounts) as the starting point. Since by definition all churches are bound by the Gospel, any organic entity that is not unified by the Gospel is not a church, but merely a religious "club."

We stress again, however: the Ephesian church was not in danger of losing their status as a church because of false doctrine, but rather because of lack of love. Lovelessness can kill a church quicker than cluelessness.

In the Spirit's closing words to Jesus' message, we see two key theological elements. The concept of "overcoming," and the mention of the tree of life. For the former, the need for genuine believers to "overcome" stands in stark contrast to the fake overcomers, the Nicolaitans, who thought they were "Overcomers" (the Greek word for "Nicolaitan" is actually based off of the word *nikaō*, the same word in v. 7). Jesus and the Spirit are essentially saying, "I hate the doctrine of those so-called 'Victory People,' but to the person who truly gains the Victory, the tree of life awaits!"

This concept of "overcoming/gaining the victory" represents a major theme in Revelation. A statement regarding "the one who

---

1 *JETS* 45.1 (March 2002): 59–72.
2 Osborne, *Revelation*, 125.

overcomes" appears in *every single letter* to the seven churches. Elsewhere in Revelation, the same Greek word *nikaō* is used in reference to the Lamb himself "overcoming" or "gaining victory over" the sealed book (5:5), and also over all the forces set in array against him (17:14), *because* he is the ultimate Sovereign.

Most fascinating, however, is how the word is used to describe the ongoing conflict between believers and the Beast. On the one hand, in both 11:7 and 13:7, the Beast, a.k.a. the Antichrist, is allowed to "conquer" (*nikaō*) believers (the two witnesses/martyrs in the former passage, and saints in general in the latter). However, juxtaposed with this stands two declarations that martyred believers have actually conquered both the Dragon and the Beast! First, in 12:11, the Dragon, Satan, as "the accuser" (one of the meanings of the Hebrew term *śātān*), is cast out of heaven, and a great voice declares that Christians "conquer" (*nikaō*) Satan through the power of the blood of the Lamb and their "word of testimony." Later, in 15:2, John himself sees a great throng of people singing "the song of Moses" and "the song of the Lamb" on a sea of brilliant, fiery glass. This throng is described as those who "had conquered the beast and his image and his mark." In other words, mere mortal humans, if they are willing to lay down their life for the Lamb, themselves conquer and overcome the Dragon and the Beast.

Thus on the one hand reference to those who "conquer" and "overcome" specifically points to martyrs, those who gave their life because of their allegiance to the Lamb. In other words, we have an ironic reversal: *by dying, you conquer!* Even today, in certain areas, Christian men and women (and sometimes children) are set on fire, beheaded, gunned down, sometimes after being horribly abused, simply because they bear the name "Christian." As far as Jesus is concerned, these martyrs are greater conquerors than Napoleon, Genghis Khan, or Julius Caesar. Those earthly "conquerors" saved their lives at first but ultimately lost them. Yet Christians, by losing their lives, conquer all enemies of the Gospel through the blood of the Lamb.

On the other hand, the directive to "conquer" seems to be directed at all Christians, not just those in a position to lose their lives. As we have seen, the last portion of each letter to the seven churches promises eternal life to those who overcome; the language is, for the most part, associated with being saved (with a couple exceptions): "the tree of life" (2:7), not being harmed by the second death (2:11), a "new name" (2:17), ruling over the nations (2:26–28; cf. 1 Corinthians 6:3, which clearly refers to all believers); white raiment and a place in the book of life (Revelation 3:5); a place in God's temple and the New Jerusalem (3:12); and the right to sit with Jesus on his throne (3:21).

A brief point must be made regarding who, exactly, makes up this group of "Overcomers." If John's own theology is to be our guide, then 1 John 5:4 gives us the key: the "one who overcomes the world" (which is a major theme of Revelation) is not some "super-Christian" or "sanctified Christian," but quite simply the one who is "born of God." The text is explicit: *everybody*—not "some of" or "the super-Christians who are," but "everybody who is born of God overcomes (present tense of *nikaō*) the world." The rest of the verse uses two more related words to demonstrate that "faith" is the "victory" (noun form of the verb *nikaō*) that "overcomes" the world. Most likely, when John in Revelation speaks of those who "overcome," he must be referring to those who are "born-again" (and John 5:4 provides no qualification, such as "born-again, if they are super-spiritual"). Furthermore, Revelation 2:11, as we shall see, declares that the overcoming one will avoid the Second Death. Revelation 21:7–8 then places a clear and obvious dichotomy between the "Overcomer" and the "Sinner." The former will forever be God's child while the latter, those who have not had their sins dealt with, will experience the Second Death (the Lake of Fire). There is no room for a middle-ground, a sort of "second-class believer." One is either an Overcomer or one is an Unbeliever.

Granted, we must avoid the shallow Christianity of "easy-believism" (i.e., "I said this prayer and can now live however I want to and still be an 'overcomer'"). Furthermore, this still begs the question of how exactly one can know they are an overcomer, and what role perseverance (which, after all, is a major theme in Revelation) plays. We cannot answer these questions here, so I will simply close the discussion by reiterating that, however we develop our theology in this regard, "overcoming" is inextricably linked to being "born of God."

So why, then, do "those who overcome/conquer" get to eat from the tree of life? In Genesis 2, in the Garden of Eden, man and woman had access to every tree God made (including the tree of life), except for the Tree of the Knowledge of Good and Evil (Genesis 2:8–9, 16–17). Yet when humanity sinned by eating from the latter, God removed access to the Tree of Life. Consequently, what we see in Revelation 2:7 is the promise of immortality to true believers, the reversal of the curse of Eden. Furthermore, in Revelation 22:1–3, the curse placed on Adam and Eve is reversed and the tree of life makes a grand reappearance in the new capital of God's creation, the New Jerusalem. Here those loyal to the Lamb, from all nations, languages, and ethnicities, will walk in the garden of this Great City and be healed by the tree of life.

In other words, when Adam and Eve sinned, they lost access to eternal life and their bodies began to corrupt: "paradise lost," to borrow John Milton's famous title. God's promise to those who overcome, however, is "paradise regained"—*not* "heaven" in the sense of "floating around up on clouds in spirit form" (this absolutely misses the point of "eternal life"), but rather *resurrected bodies* that can taste of the tree of life without fear of judgment.

The Spirit's mention of the tree of life goes beyond the obvious reference to Genesis 2–3, however. As Colin Hemer shows us, the Artemis Temple in Ephesus had its own "tree of life," the olive tree near which Artemis herself was supposedly born. Indeed, the Ephesians celebrated this holy site with a yearly festival, at least up until the time of Strabo (d. early 1st century AD). In fact, "The numismatic evidence suffices to show that the tree, like the bee and the stag, was distinctively associated with Artemis Ephesia."[1]

---

1 Hemer, *Letters to the Seven Churches of Asia*, 45–47.

So we see that the first mention of the tree of life in Revelation is specifically directed at the one church that would have been constantly reminded of a pagan "tree of life" on the grounds of the greatest symbol of idolatry in Asia Minor. The Spirit, then, intends to contrast God's "tree of life" with Artemis.[1] Artemis' "tree of life" was set in its own "paradise garden" of sorts, and served as a sanctuary for the guilty.[2] Hemer aptly sums up the situation:

> For the Christian in Domitianic Ephesus these thoughts would, I suggest, have come to a focus in a contemporary reality. The words of the epistle contrasted with a shocking parody which the pagan cult of the city offered. At the heart of its changing fortunes was the theocratic power of the Artemis temple, marked by the fixed point of the ancient tree-shrine, which was the place of 'salvation' for the suppliant, surrounded by an asylum enclosed by a boundary wall. But this 'salvation' for the criminal corrupted the city. The Ephesian who had to live with this problem understood the promise of a city-sanctuary pervaded by the glory of God. Of that city it was said, 'There shall in no wise enter into it anything that defileth, neither whatsoever worketh abomination, or maketh a lie' (Rev. 21:27)."[3]

Thus, in the midst of the moral depravity centered around the "paradise" of Artemis' cult—a tree that testified to a man-made construct rather than the eternal God, a sanctuary that offered safety to the wicked but not salvation, a wall that kept wickedness in instead of out, and a "garden" that facilitated the disease of sin instead of healing—in the midst of this satanic counterfeit, the Spirit assures believers that a greater City awaits, a City where the redeemed of all ages and ethnicities can walk in safety. In the midst of all this stands the Cross, the "tree of life" where all the wickedness of those enslaved to Artemis was carried by the Lamb himself, and

---

1 Ibid., 45–46.
2 Ibid., 48–50.
3 Ibid., 51.

overcome, so that the Ephesians could turn from Artemis' fake paradise and walk forever in the paradise of God.[1]

QUESTIONS FOR FURTHER DISCUSSION

1. What are some ways in which it might be easy to "lose your first love"? How can this be prevented?
2. At what point does one cross the line from "hating heresy" to "hating heretics"? How can this be avoided?
3. What are the key doctrines over which Christians cannot disagree? How should these be defended?
4. What, today, is the greatest symbol (or symbols) of pagan idolatry, and how should Christians react against it?

---

[1] Hemer develops this interesting train of thought by connecting the "Tree of Life" in Revelation to Jesus on the cross: Thus, "We may see the Ephesian Christian as finding a picture of refuge in the presence of the Christ who died on the tree, a 'salvation' which he might appropriate only there, and an adoption into the citizenship of the kingdom for the repentant sinner and outsider" (Ibid., 52).

5

SMYRNA—
FEAR NOT
THE PERSECUTOR

July 28th, 1974: Xinglongchang, China. Members of the Christian community "The Little Flock of the Narrow Gate" (most if not all from the A-Hmao ethnic minority) pray together in the bowels of a cave as communist troops approach. Five years earlier communist officials had come to one of their villages, confronted each head of the household, and demanded to know who they were loyal to. Their response? "On earth we rely on Chairman Mao, but spiritually we give our allegiance to God." This failed to satisfy the government officials, and an era of persecution began. The Communists took away their ability to work the land, eliminated "their monthly salt ration and clothing coupons," and tortured the leader of this church.[1] Paul Hattaway describes their plight:

> Rejected by their country, the Christians of Xiaoshiqiao struggled to survive. They roamed the forest eating wild herbs and fruit. Some dwelt in isolated caves. Many of them died, especially the young children and the elderly who were not able to endure the hardship. Nothing, however, could shake the Christians' resolve.[2]

Yet their number began to grow, and soon the Communists saw them as a significant threat to the government. On that fateful day in 1974, as many of them were praying in a cave, Communist

---

[1] Paul Hattaway, *China's Book of Martyrs: AD 845–Present*, vol. 1 of *The Church in China* (Carlisle, CA: Piquant, 2007), 539–541.
[2] Ibid., 539.

troops slaughtered them.[1] "Of whom the world was not worthy ..." (Hebrews 11:38).

Today, I picture those believers standing under the altar with future martyrs in Revelation 6:10, asking why God's justice is delayed. Revelation, like other books of the Bible, grapples with the question of why bad things happen to God's people. The letter to Smyrna in Revelation 2:8–11 does not actually answer that question, but instead offers hope: those who suffer for the crucified and resurrected Messiah receive a "crown of life."

THE BACKGROUND OF SMYRNA

If Ephesus was the cosmopolitan "New York" of Asia Minor, then Smyrna was the proud "Boston." She claimed, among other things, to be the birthplace of the venerable Homer himself (a claim contested by other cities, of course!), and called herself "First in Asia."[2] In addition, a well-known historian named Hermogenes had graced the city with an epic, two-volume history of Smyrna.[3] Indeed, considering the fact that Smyrna alone of our seven cities has survived as a major city to this day (as the modern Izmir),[4] perhaps she does indeed have more legitimate historical relevance than her rivals!

The name "Smyrna" itself seems to have come from a local tree that "produces a resin from which myrrh was made for perfume or embalming."[5] In addition, Smyrna was gorgeous, and knew it. Famous orators and writers such as Aelius Aristides and Apollonius of Tyana proclaimed her beauty—not her natural beauty, but her architecture.[6] Indeed, "The ancient sense of beauty extolled the buildings and their arrangement …. It is as a harmonious archi-

---

1 Ibid., 540.
2 Osborne, *Revelation*, 127.
3 Hemer, *Letters to the Seven Churches of Asia*, 57.
4 Osborne, *Revelation*, 127.
5 Gary M. Burge, Lynn H. Cohick, and Gene L. Green, *The New Testament in Antiquity* (Grand Rapids, MI: Zondervan, 2009), 429.
6 Hemer, *Letters to the Seven Churches of Asia*, 58–59.

tectural whole that Aristides likens the city to a flower and to a statue."[1] In addition, the term "crown" was often used as a simile for Smyrna, apparently "Originat[ing] in the physical appearance of the city rising symmetrically to its 'crown' of battlements."[2]

Smyrna lay just 35 miles to the north of her sister Ephesus, and like her sister was a harbor city with vigorous trade.[3] In addition, her loyalty to Rome was undisputed, lauded by Greco-Roman historians Tacitus and Livy.[4] Indeed, Smyrna was the first to build a temple dedicated to the goddess *Roma* (almost 300 years earlier), "and in A.D. 26, because of its long loyalty to Rome, it beat out ten other cities for the privilege of building a temple to the emperor Tiberius."[5] In other words, Smyrna represented what every city in the empire wanted to be: rich, beautiful, and utterly devoted to her master, Rome.

Jesus' Message to Smyrna

Jesus' messages to Smyrna and Philadelphia are the only two letters without any negative critique. This does not mean, of course, that these the churches were perfect, but rather that they had not allowed false doctrines, compromise, and arrogant attitudes to infiltrate them like the other churches, and that they had not allowed zeal for true doctrine to result in lack of love.

To the believers at Smyrna, Jesus encourages them that he is both "the first and the last" as well as the Resurrected One (1:8). The former designation echoes the language of 1:8, 11, but it does more than that. Recall that Smyrna considered herself "#1," the best of Asia, the beauty queen of the competition and "trophy wife" of Caesar himself. It was at her hands that Christians in Smyrna were suffering, and so Jesus reminds them that He alone is #1.[6] As proof

---

1 Ibid., 59.
2 Ibid.
3 Osborne, *Revelation*, 127.
4 Hemer, *Letters to the Seven Churches of Asia*, 70–71.
5 Osborne, *Revelation*, 127.
6 Ibid., 128.

of Jesus' superiority, he mentions his resurrection, indicating the worthiness of the Lamb and the validity of his claims (cf. 1:17–19).

As far as the world is concerned, the primary characteristics of this church are that she is persecuted and poor (2:9), hardly a community worth emulating! Indeed, one gets a picture here of the rich "popular girl," Smyrna, the homecoming queen dating the football team's quarterback (Caesar), turning up her nose and bullying the "poor girl," the church. Such, indeed, is the way of the world: money and popularity mean power and social status. Prestige gives us an opportunity to act in a certain way: to strut, to speak condescendingly, to make sure we get the best of what's on the table. Sadly, this has been a problem even within the church (James 2:1–6; 1 Corinthians 11:21–22), and even today many go around promoting material possessions as the superior sign of God's blessing.

Yet this view of material possessions as "blessing" stands in direct opposition to a key biblical truth: God has decreed that "the *poor* of this world" will be "rich in faith and heirs of the kingdom" (James 2:5). Indeed, while Jesus' followers were to be willing to sell all they had to give to the poor, the otherwise moral rich young man who was not willing to do so was denied entrance into the Kingdom by Jesus himself (Mark 10:21–23). This stands in stark opposition to the attitude of the world. As far as the city of Smyrna is concerned, the small church within her gates is "poor," and thus deserved ridicule. However, in Jesus' eyes, the situation is reversed: the church in Smyrna is actually rich! Here Jesus lays out for us one of the key truths in Scripture: faith, not money, makes one rich. In other words, the church at Smyrna is "more than meets the eye."

Furthermore, as we shall see later, the church at Smyrna stands in stark contrast with Laodicea, the "rich" church. The latter, on the basis of her outward prosperity, thought that she needed nothing. Smyrna, on the other hand, recognizes that she has nothing left but Jesus. Thus her faith is enabled, amplified; like the Apostle Paul, she is at the point where she can declare that Jesus' grace is sufficient for her.

Where Is Your Allegiance?

What a challenge, then, for North American churches when we think that a fancy building, an overflowing offering, our prestige within the community, and the "cutting-edge fashion" that our members exhibit is somehow indicative of our value in God's eyes! In reality, the poorer a church is, the more opportunity they have to rely upon God. A church that depends always on the grace of God, like that in Smyrna, offers a much more powerful message to her community than a church that "has it made."

Yet the threat facing this community of believers cannot be minimized. Apparently, the Jews of the city were leading the offense in slandering them to the authorities (2:8). In the Roman empire, the Jews possessed a special dispensation to not worship the emperor or other gods; so long as Christians were considered Jews, they enjoyed the same privilege. Yet sometimes the officials could not tell the difference between Christian Jews and non-Christian Jews, and so both were punished (this may be the reason Jews, not just Christians, were kicked out of Rome in Acts 18:2; cf. the historian Suetonius, *Claudius* 25). Quite possibly, to protect the best interests of their community, influential Jews "had become active in instigating persecution of the church or denouncing to the authorities those Jews who were also Christians."[1]

This does not, however, make either John or Jesus, both Jews, anti-Semitic. Here Jesus, the Jew, is not suggesting any inferiority or inherent evil within Jews themselves, only that by opposing the followers of Jesus Christ, they were denying their own heritage (thus echoing his own words in John 8:42–44). Furthermore, generally speaking the "villains" of Revelation, those who would oppose the Lamb and persecute her followers, are not Jews (Revelation 3:9 notwithstanding), while some of the "heroes" are clearly Jews (Revelation 7:4–9). Furthermore, as we have noted earlier in Revelation 1:7 (citing Zechariah 12:10), John makes it clear that all humanity bears equal blame acting as "Christ-killers" (yet all humanity may conversely share in the hope of the Messiah).

---

1 Hemer, *Letters to the Seven Churches of Asia*, 67–68.

Nevertheless, as Ben Witherington points out, "Whatever human agencies were involved, John clearly places the ultimate blame on Satan. He is the one who casts them into prison."[1] Through the influence of Satan, Smyrna's believers will be thrown into prison for "10 days" (which may be a literal 10 days, or simply shorthand for an indeterminate yet relatively short period of time). Interestingly, the Roman Empire generally did not utilize "prisons" for permanent incarceration, i.e., as punishment in of itself, but rather for short-term incarceration leading up to a trial or an execution.[2] This, then, explains why Jesus urges the believers of Smyrna to be "faithful to death." The "10-day period" would not involve merely twiddling one's thumbs in prison until the term of punishment was over, but meant, for many, Roman execution.

The Roman empire, like modern society, enjoyed its athletic competitions and idolized her athletes. As is well known, athletes received a "crown" consisting of a wreath of vegetation about their head. Public adulation accompanied such "crowning." In contrast, those led out to a public death represent the antithesis of the athlete: public humiliation rather than reverence. Yet in a powerful reversal, the King of Kings declares that these poor spectacles of derision receive the "real" crown.

Believers, then, represent a radical contrast with the city herself. The city is gorgeous, rich and influential, perfumed and basking in the adoration of her lover, Caesar. She herself is a "crown." Furthermore, even her influential dead received "crowns" posthumously.[3] Christians in Smyrna, however, are poor, downtrodden, bullied, and harassed on every side. No public adulation from the crowd awaits them, but only the threat of public execution. Yet, in the eyes of Jesus, they are conquering heroes, "overcomers," who will receive a "crown of life," not a crown posthumously like the best of Smyrna would expect.[4]

---

1 Witherington, *Revelation*, 101.
2 Hemer, *Letters to the Seven Churches of Asia*, 68.
3 Ibid., 73.
4 Ibid., 74.

Key to Jesus' encouragement of the downtrodden believers is his command to "not fear" what will happen to them at the hands of the devil's minions (2:10a). This echoes Jesus' command to John in 1:17, where the imperative is based on the person and work of Jesus Christ: "Do not fear *because* of who I am and what I've done." Similarly, the command to believers in 2:10 hinges on the ability of Jesus Christ to provide "a crown of life." Believers must not fear, then, because, as John eloquently states in one of his epistles, "You have conquered [*nikaō*!] them because the one in you is greater than the one in the world" (1 John 4:4). Relying on Jesus Christ and his accomplishments frees us from the "punishing" effect of fear (1 John 4:18).

Interestingly, however, we see a tension in Revelation (and the rest of Scripture) between the command *not* to fear and the assumption that believers *should* fear God himself (Revelation 11:18, 14:7, 15:4, 19:5, cf. Matthew 10:28—all passages which use the same Greek word as Revelation 1:17 and 2:10). So what is "fear" and why should we *not* fear the ones persecuting us, but fear God instead? The latter is a very important question, since many Christians grew up in a home dominated by a parent who, instead of love, instilled a tormenting, punishing fear into the home.

The issue, unfortunately, cannot be addressed satisfactorily at this point. Suffice it to say that, on the one hand, Jesus does not want his loyal followers cowering in fear, unsure of what horrors await them. In Revelation 1:17, when John falls down in terror before the incredible picture before him, Jesus Christ admonishes him to not fear on the basis of Jesus' own identity (1:17b–18).

On the other hand, "fear" in the Bible can also point to the awe and reverence that God and the Lamb are worthy of. This is the opposite of flippancy: when ushered into the presence of the King, the appropriate response is not a "high-five" but rather bowing the knee in reverence (Ephesians 3:14). This type of "fear" is not the opposite of love; to the contrary, love for God and fear of God go hand in hand, for such a "fear" is not punished by anxiety over what will happen or how God will react towards me, but rather consists of an incredible depth of awe at the power of God to accomplish in me the miracle of Salvation.[1] Consequently, while unhealthy fear is a fear of the unknown, often tied to the evil character of a particular person or group of people, healthy "fear" in the New Testament, especially Revelation, equals the awe and reverence directed at the mighty God who loves his people.

Finally, we have the closing statement in 2:11b that the victorious one will not experience "The Second Death." This verse introduces what will become a major theme in Revelation, namely the extreme danger that the unrepentant inhabitants of the world are in. The Second Death in Revelation is contrasted to "normal" death, such as those facing the believers in Smyrna (cf. also Revelation 12:11). This Second Death, however, is also contrasted with the "First Resurrection" in Revelation 20:6—those who experience the latter will not experience the former. In Revelation 20:13–14 and 21:8 the Second Death is explicitly identified with the Lake of Fire, and those who belong there are those sinners (21:8) who do not have their name written down in the Book of Life (20:15). Those who are written in the Book of Life, however, do not experience death ever again (Revelation 21:4).

So who, exactly, is the "one who overcomes," i.e., the "victorious one"? I do not, in this book, wish to delve into theological debate about the nature of perseverance or whether or not one can "lose their salvation." I acknowledge on the one hand that the mantra "once-saved-always-saved" can become a license to sin if left to itself, and "easy-believism" is a threat to every Christian generation. On the other hand, the security of the believer in Jesus Christ apart from any merit of his or her own should not be easily dismissed, either (e.g., John 10:29, 1 Peter 1:5).

---

1   Discussions of the concept of "fear" in Christian scholarly literature are rare, though in my research I was especially intrigued by Daniel Estes, "Poetic Artistry in the Expression of Fear in Psalm 49," *BibSac* 161 (Jan 2004): 55–71, and John F. Bettler, "Guidelines from II Timothy for Counseling People with Fear," *WTJ* 26.2 (1974): 198–208.

I have already briefly dealt with the "overcoming one" in Johannine theology. I will simply add here that in Revelation the one who overcomes the world would seem simply to be the one who identifies with Jesus instead of the Beast. Consequently, the call in Revelation to "be victorious" seems to be a call to ascertain that one is identified with Jesus Christ (namely, as we saw in 1 John, that one is "born of God," or, from John 3, "born-again").

Yet this is not automatically assumed simply because one belongs to a church! Indeed, Jesus doles out some very harsh warnings to those within the church; in 2:16 he threatens so-called believers, associated with the Nicolaitans, with open warfare by the Son himself, and 2:20–23, specifically, demands repentance from those associated with Jezebel. The implication seems to be that such people will not be "overcomers" if they continue on their current trajectory (it must be pointed out here, however, that it is *Jesus alone* who can pass judgment on one's soul; the rest of us should certainly be calling people back to an examination of themselves, but only Jesus reserves the right to pass final judgment).

To be an "overcomer," then is to place pure allegiance to Jesus Christ over the calls of the world, whether they be the call to turn aside from Christ and become more socially acceptable (Smyrna), or the call towards a compromising, pagan syncretism which, in the end, stands in opposition to Jesus Christ (Pergamum and Thyatira). Individual churches may have unique threats to their allegiance to Jesus Christ. The Lamb warns them, lest they suddenly find out that not all of them are truly "born of God." For such people that feign initial allegiance to the Lamb but ultimately turn away to the siren calls of the world, it would have been better for them not to have heard the truth in the first place (cf. 2 Peter 2:20–21).

The true overcomer may expect opposition and even abuse. In March 1995, a thirty-six-year-old Chinese woman named Wu Xiuling died at home. Her death came as the result of hard work in a labor camp where failure to meet a quota resulted in violent abuse. She had been arrested first in 1989, in Zhao Village (Shandong Province, near Zaozhuang), for being a follower of Jesus Christ and also for preaching from Revelation, "a book especially feared by the Chinese authorities."[1] The second time she was arrested, 1993, led to her physical deterioration and death two years later. Near the point of death, she is described in this manner: "Her bones were just under the skin, and her face was distorted. Her skinny hand became transparent and the bones could be seen. Her face did not show any trace of blood colour, eyes deeply sunk back."[2]

What a sight! Who could look at Wu Xiuling and see anything glamorous? Who could possibly look at her and see the hand of God? Yet what God sees and what humans see are two different things. The state of Wu Xiuling offers us some surprising parallels to how the Apostle Paul describes himself in 2 Corinthians 4:7–10.[3] Paul himself recognized that, in the eyes of many in the Corinthian church, his physical state could not possibly reflect God's blessing. As an evangelist friend of mine has pointed out, many in the Corinthian church were essentially saying, "If Paul is truly doing God's work, then how'd he end up looking like death warmed-over? We'd expect a bit better from God's emissary." No doubt the Corinthians would have said the same of Wu Xiuling.

Yet Paul, in verse 11, gives us the answer to the Corinthian's wrong perspective: the physical abuse the Apostle Paul (and Wu Xiuling, and many others) suffered occurs *specifically so that the life of Jesus might be manifest* to all those around him (both to the Corinthian believers and unbelievers). Far from being a sign of God's displeasure, Paul's beaten physical state, which at times seems to have been on the verge of death (v.11a), nevertheless bears *testimony* to Jesus Christ, just as Jesus' broken (and later resurrected) body bore testimony to God the Father.

---

1 Hattaway, *China's Book of Martyrs*, 578.
2 Ibid.
3 I am indebted to a sermon by evangelist Bobby Bosler, "The Comfort Continuum," on Second Corinthians, preached November 1st, 2016, at the Baptist College of Ministry chapel, for stimulating my thinking here. Much of the material in the next few sentences and the next paragraph was significantly influenced by his sermon.

Where Is Your Allegiance?

Neither the description of Wu Xiuling, given above, nor the description of the Apostle Paul in 2 Corinthians 4 are "glamorous." As far as the world is concerned, they are worthy of nothing but being snubbed. As far as the Lamb is concerned, they are the most beautiful images in his mosaic: "They will be mine," the Father declares, "when I myself make them my treasure" (Malachi 3:17).[1]

QUESTIONS FOR FURTHER DISCUSSION

1. What do you, personally, know of persecuted Christians? Have you ever prayed for any specifically? What steps can you take to ensure that such Christians are always present in your prayers?
2. What unique challenges might face Christians in a church like that in Smyrna? What steps could such Christians take to ensure that they stay true to the faith in the midst of discouragement?

---

[1] My own translation. KJV has "… when I make up my jewels"; NIV has "… they will be my treasured possession."

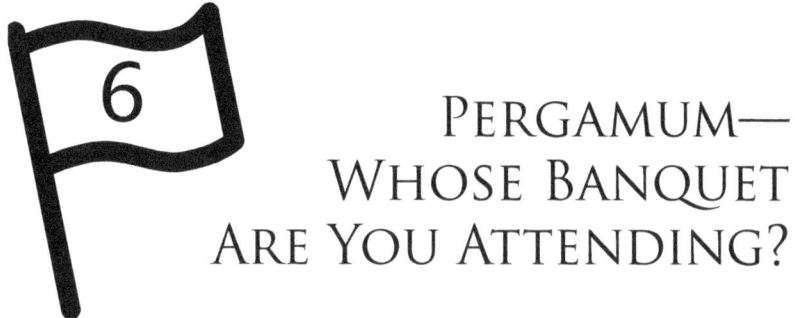

PERGAMUM— WHOSE BANQUET ARE YOU ATTENDING?

In the misty twilight of the evening, a grandiose temple in the heart of an Anatolian city brims with laughter and reveling. Burning lamps flicker and illuminate the marble pillars of the structure. The spirit of Bacchus is hard at work: the wine flows freely, the sacred prostitutes strut brazenly, and the best spices and meats set one's mouth watering. The rich and powerful of the city mingle, their lips brimming with political gossip and business boastings. At the center of it all sit three edifices dedicated to the emperor Domitian, Zeus, and the serpent god Asklepios. Reverence will be given, and the meat of the meal will be offered first to the entities represented by those three shrines. The Christian, standing outside the steps of the *portico* leading to the entrance, pauses to ponder whether or not he should even be there. Under the curious eyes of the slaves at the entrance, the Christian weighs the social expectations of the feast (after all, he's a member of the guild; his colleagues *expect* him to be there!) against the blatant paganism. Does Jesus truly expect him to give up this opportunity? Hasn't he already suffered enough mockery from his colleagues due to his association with these "Jesus freaks"! What's the harm with one little party?

THE BACKGROUND OF PERGAMUM

Approximately seventy miles north of Smyrna and over a thousand feet above the Caicus River, a great citadel towered above yet another magnificent city competing for the emperor's affections;

this one, however, could boast a university, residing Attalic princes, and the production of popular *pergamena* parchment for writing.[1] Claiming as her founder the Arcadian hero Telephus (who assisted the Greeks in the famous conquest of Troy), Pergamum, along with Smyrna and Ephesus, competed in their drive to honor Rome and the emperor. To a certain degree, Pergamum could claim victory. In 29 BC Ceasar Augustus gave the nod to the creation of temples dedicated both to himself and to *Roma* here at Pergamum, boosting the city's claim to "primacy in the imperial cult" and thus becoming a model for other Anatolian cities (Pergamum's temple was, in fact, depicted on some of the city's coins).[2]

The pride of Pergamum was her pagan piety. In addition to her emperor worship, an elaborate altar forty-feet tall, dedicated to Zeus, threatened to "shock-and-awe" any visitors. For those bored with the "king of gods," altars to Athena, Dionysus, and the serpentine Asklepios also awaited reverence.[3] Naturally, those objects of reverence played key roles in various feasts, social functions where the important could mingle.

Significantly, out of all these objects of worship, Zeus, Asklepion, and the Roman Emperor all claimed the title of "Savior." In fact, Nero was especially known for the titles "savior of the world" and "Lord of all the Cosmos," while Domitian was hailed as "*dominus et deus*," or "Lord and god."[4] This was not mere lip service; much of the characteristics of the city itself were "subordinated to the emperor's authority and cult," with festivals in honor of the emperor playing a significant role in the city; in other words, "cultic life" (devotion to the emperor and other gods) often merged with "city life."[5]

---

1 Hemer, *Letters to the Seven Churches of Asia*, 79–84, 86–87; Osborne, *Revelation*, 138–139; John F. Walvoord, *The Revelation of Jesus Christ* (Chicago: Moody, 1966), 65–66.
2 Hemer, *Letters to the Seven Churches of Asia*, 84.
3 Osborne, *Revelation*, 139.
4 Hemer, *Letters to the Seven Churches of Asia*, 82, 86–87.
5 Hemer, *Letters to the Seven Churches of Asia*, 92.

JESUS' MESSAGE TO PERGAMUM

In the previous chapter, we saw how Jesus Christ offers strong encouragement and blessing to those who persevere under pressure, especially physical persecution. From the American Christian who faces ridicule and mockery to her face and behind her back, to the Chinese pastor imprisoned for holding a church meeting with over a certain number of attendees, to the Indian Christian set on fire by radical Hindus—these all are truly victorious, and are more likely than others to possess the grandest seats at the Marriage Supper of the Lamb.

Yet sadly, in this chapter we learn that even though a persecuted church has a special place in God's heart, this does not necessarily absolve them from Jesus' rebuke. To the contrary, as we see from the opening words of the letter, "he who has the sharp two-edged sword," this will not be a pleasant encounter between the Lamb and his church, no matter how well they have borne under pressure.[1] This "double-edged sword" was, on the one hand, a "symbol of Roman justice," a broadsword originating in Thrace and adapted for the empire's use (though Jesus may also be alluding to Isaiah 11:4 here). Yet Jesus makes it clear that it is not the local Roman governor's power they need to be afraid of; the church answers to the Jewish Messiah, and him alone![2] This functions as both a comfort and a warning. A comfort, for on the one hand no earthly power, whether Roman or Greek, can sever them from the almighty hand of God. Yet a warning also, since offending the Jewish Messiah, the Lamb exalted above all other thrones and powers, is far more frightening than offending the Roman Emperor.

The good news is that the believers at Pergamum, like those in Smyrna, have persevered under pressure. They have done so despite living in the shadow of the "throne of Satan." What Jesus specifically means by that phrase is unknown for sure; we have already mentioned how Pergamaum was steeped in idolatry, so there were

---

1   Witherington, *Revelation*, 102.
2   Osborne, *Revelation*, 140.

more than enough satanic shrines to go around. The city was full of "thrones." However, Hemer and Osborne both see the Imperial cult as the best candidate,[1] and I would concur. Each city had its own patron deities, but only the Emperor was meant to be universally revered, and we have already noted how Pergamum zealously tried to outstrip the other cities in its adoration of Caesar. Hemer, then, is certainly correct when he states, "The claims of Caesar are viewed by John as a Satanic parody of those of Christ."[2]

Right there in the middle of "Satan's hometown,"[3] then, the believers continue to proclaim their loyalty to Jesus Christ. Indeed, the word Jesus uses here is significant, for it is not the normal word for "have" or "possess." Instead, he says that the believers "grasp" or "seize" or even "cling to" (Greek *krateō*) the name of Jesus, perhaps similar to how one would seize a lifeline in the raging sea. They recognize that the name of Jesus does not allow half-hearted loyalty in the face of danger; they refuse to deny his faith. Furthermore, one of their own, Antipas, has already paid the ultimate penalty, and consequently is given a title nobody else in the New Testament has, a title that echoes Jesus' own identity—"My witness, my faithful one." For all their flaws, these believers possess true grit and also a genuine all-star (Antipas) worth emulating.

As if to underscore the point that Jesus knows their difficulties, he mentions once again, "the place where Satan dwells"; the verb "dwell" (Greek *katoikeō*) becomes a frame for the positive part of Jesus' performance review ("where you dwell . . where Satan dwells"; 2:13). They are worthy of praise specifically because the devil has "home field advantage," and yet they have not given up.

As a side note, if we are correct in assuming that "Satan" here is manifested in the Imperial Cult, this underscores the nature of the future antichrist (and, indeed, all true antichrists; cf. 1 John 2:18). An antichrist is one who sets himself up as worthy of devo-

---

1 Hemer, *Letters to the Seven Churches of Asia*, 86–87; Osborne, *Revelation*, 141.
2 Hemer, *Letters to the Seven Churches of Asia*, 87.
3 Osborne, *Letters to the Seven Churches of Asia*, 143.

tion instead of ("*anti*") Jesus Christ, thus denying Jesus' name (i.e., authority). The Beast in Revelation, just like the Roman Emperor, encourages, even *demands*, reverence that belongs only to the Lamb. Yet the true Christian, like those in Pergamum, not only acknowledges his or her relationship with Jesus, his or her loyalty to the Name, but also is not ashamed to trumpet Jesus' ultimate royalty over all prima donnas and imperial wannabees. Such was this church's strength.

Now the bad news: perseverance under pressure does not give one a free pass for theological compromise. Despite their excellent handling of *external* problems, they have not appropriately handled *internal* problems—they were allowing within their own community of faith those who would corrupt it.

The language here is fascinating: having commended the believers for "grasping" (*krateō*) onto the name of Jesus, he uses the exact same word to describe the false teachers in their midst: they are "grasping" (*krateō*) onto the teaching of Balaam and the teaching of the Nicolaitans. For all practical purposes, these two groups are the same (the first three Greek words of verse 15 seem to indicate this).[1] In other words, we can better understand these Nicolaitans by understanding who Balaam was in the Old Testament. Although initially Balaam blessed Israel (Numbers 22–24), we see a surprising fact in Numbers 31:8 and 16—Israel executed Balaam because he was instrumental in advising Moab how to cause Israel to sin and thus invoke God's wrath. In the "Peor incident," recorded in Numbers 25, the Moabites (under the council of Balaam), invite Israel to "the sacrifices of their gods." However, these "sacrifices" were not spectator sports, like tourists visiting a temple. Rather, this passage tells us three things, all of which have their own equivalent in the Greco-Roman festivals: the Israelites fornicated with Moabite women (perhaps even "sacred" prostitutes), ate the food there at the festival, and gave reverence to the pagan gods. Consequently, according to Numbers 25:3, Israel "yoked them-

---

1 Osborne, *Revelation*, 145.

selves to the Baal of Peor" (NIV).[1] The result was sudden, bloody judgment. Israel had been fooled into thinking that the holy people of God could "party with the pagans"—feasting combined with immorality and idolatry—and remain unscathed.

Ever since then, the name "Balaam" became synonymous with sinful compromise (cf. 2 Peter 2:15; Jude 11). By linking the Nicolaitans with the name "Balaam," Jesus is warning, "In the same way that Balaam subverted the Israelites, these false teachers are trying to subvert you."[2] While the exact characteristics of the idolatry had changed, the principle was still the same. In light of the expression "things sacrificed unto idols," Jesus is warning against the "dinner parties" which included "meat sacrificed and then eaten in the presence of an idol, which is to say within a pagan temple," while the immorality would refer to the "sacred prostitutes" or, more generally, to "the sexual dalliance that went on at dinner parties held in the temple precincts."[3] The idolatry, of course, would include reverence towards Caesar as well as other pagan gods: "The heretics were apparently teaching that there was nothing wrong with participating in the imperial cult, since even most Romans did it out of civic duty rather than actual worship.... Most likely actual idolatry took place, possibly temple feasts in honor of 'Caesar, god and savior.'"[4]

The interaction of Christians with the world has been a difficult issue for the church for nearly 2,000 years. What, exactly, is "worldly"? What will cause one's "testimony" to be harmed? In some cases, the questions are legitimate and need to be puzzled through humbly. Yet here, in his letter to Pergamum, the Lamb makes it absolutely clear that there is a line that cannot be crossed, no matter how sumptuous the fare: idolatry and all its trappings.

---

1 I cite the NIV here because this version appropriately brings out the picturesque sense of the Hebrew word "yoke" that other versions neglect.
2 Osborne, *Revelation*, 144–145.
3 Witherington, *Revelation*, 103.
4 Osborne, *Revelation*, 144.

Where Is Your Allegiance?

Furthermore, we North American believers must not delude ourselves that simply because no pagan deities are named, that they are absent from many modern "parties." The god Bacchus does not need to be literally worshipped in order to hold sway at a party. Indeed, our cunning adversary, ever in tune with the winds of change, has simple replaced the name "Bacchus" with another one: "Pleasure." A stone altar has been replaced with a digital one and meat has been replaced with drugs. The wine is often more potent, all the better to remove inhibitions quicker. The sexuality is relatively unchanged, though perhaps more subtle. The end result is the same: a god named Pleasure is worshipped.

Believers today may very well be forced to a decision when invited to a banquet: is the pagan god Pleasure, or even Power, or even, perhaps, the more subtle goddess "Self-Promotion" presiding? Not every banquet is like that, of course. The *Imago Dei*, the image of God in humanity, pushes us to socialize with each other in appropriate ways. Food, drink, a game or two, sharing pictures and stories and humor—these reflect the social nature of the triune God. Furthermore, Jesus himself appeared at banquets with unbelievers, though something tells me the very presence of the Son of God would have chased out the presence of Bacchus.

The consequences for attending the wrong banquet—any banquet that honors a false god— is severe. Believers have no business appearing in a place where their loyalty would be put into question, any more than a Cleveland Indians fan belongs at a "Ben Zobrist Appreciation Night" in Chicago. In v. 16, Jesus, once again casually mentioning his sword, threatens to declare war on those who are encouraging this pagan synchronism. Although his anger is directed mostly against the Nicolaitans, Jesus states that he will come "to you," i.e., the church, and that they (all of them) must repent.[1] They will suffer collateral damage when Jesus goes to war, for it is they who have been tolerating the Nicolaitans in their midst. In other words, "the believers are being given a choice: go to war

---

1 Osborne, *Revelation*, 146.

against the heretics or else God will do so for them but with far more drastic results."[1]

Jesus' closing lines further develop this "banquet" theme. The "hidden manna," of course, refers back to the manna the children received in the midst of their wilderness wanderings. Jesus' point is clear: "The heavenly feast will belong to those who now abstain from the imperial *eidolothuta* [food offered to idols]."[2] Furthermore, in contrast to the emperor and all he offers, the manna represents Jesus himself. Just as John wrote in his Gospel, Jesus is the true "manna," the "bread of life" (John 6:27, 35, 48, 50–51); Revelation 2 shows us that "in contrast to food associated with false gods," Jesus Christ "satisfies his people's needs."[3]

The "white stone" is somewhat harder to identify; Hemer offers seven possible interpretations![4] However, a popular view among scholars (and one that would best fit with the context and background) is that it is "an allusion to the white pebble used in antiquity for admission to some feasts …. We should perhaps see these stones as an engraved invitation to the messianic banquet."[5] In other words, "The mana and white stones are both eschatological symbols related to the messianic feast at the eschaton …."[6] This strengthens the contrast between pagan banquets and Jesus' banquet. Both require a special graven invitation. The Nicolaitan, the "false overcomer" who is willing to compromise to enter the former type of banquet, will get his or her (temporary) fill of pleasure, but will deny Christ by his actions. The Christian, the "true overcomer," receives a personalized, graven invitation with a new name, welcoming him into the Messianic Banquet. There she will learn that fellowship with the Lamb and his followers provides a

---

1 Ibid.
2 Hemer, *Letters to the Seven Churches of Asia*, 95.
3 Daniel K. K. Wong, "The Hidden Manna and the White Stone in Revelation 2:17," *BibSac* 155 (April 1998): 348.
4 Hemer, *Letters to the Seven Churches of Asia*, 96.
5 Witherington, *Revelation*, 103–104.
6 Osborne, *Revelation*, 149.

greater pleasure than can be gained by the drunken revelries presided over by Bacchus.

The "banquet" motif plays a major role in John's theology. The very first miracle Jesus performs, in John 2, is at a wedding banquet and foreshadows his own messianic kingdom. Quite possibly John 6 builds on the "banqueting" theme of Proverbs 9, while the Gospel of John itself closes with Jesus providing a "banquet" for his disciples (John 21).[1] In Revelation 19, the "marriage supper of the Lamb" becomes a prominent theme, and this special banquet is contrasted with the "banquet" provided for carrion by the corpses of those who opposed the Lamb. This forcefully brings out the following point: everybody will attend *some* sort of banquet, but which one? The fake "overcomer" attends any banquet he or she chooses now, since Jesus Christ takes second place to social prestige or personal pleasure. In the end, however, the fake "overcomer" will be bounced from the door of the only Banquet that matters. Those who, on the other hand, are willing to endure the mockery and snobbery of the world—since their association with the Lamb matters more than any personal gain they would gain from attending pagan banquets—such a one will gain entrance to the eternal meal hosted by the eternal Bread of Life.

One more point can be added to this. In Acts 2:42, the early church is marked by four characteristics: the teaching of the apostles, fellowship, eating meals together (literally "breaking bread"), and prayers (cf. also 2:46). In other words, eating together was important to the church! The church of Jesus Christ, then, is meant to function as an alternative community, a family, where brothers and sisters enjoy each other's company. Rather than lack of inhibitions, lasciviousness, the flaunting of wealth, and worship of the emperor, the church is marked by self-control, chastity, giving to the poor (Acts 2:45, cf. Galatians 2:10), and worship of the King

---

1 For further discussion on the "banqueting" theme in John 6, see R. J. Dillon, "Wisdom Tradition and Sacramental Retrospect in the Cana Account (Jn 2,1–11)," *Catholic Biblical Quarterly* 24 (1964): 271–272, 275, 278.

of Kings. Given the choice, Christians should have no trouble deciding which banquet they prefer.

Questions for Further Discussion

1. What type of "banquets" tempt the Christian today within secular society? How can you determine whether or not a party or social function would compromise your testimony?
2. What aspects of society today (social, political, etc.) stand in stark opposition to Jesus Christ? How can the Christian "speak the truth in love" regarding those corrupt parts of society without coming across as "holier-than-thou"?
3. How can believers in the church keep each other accountable regarding moral compromises (without becoming a "busybody" or a "gossip")?

7

Thyatira—
Beware the
Rogue Prophetess

The hustle and bustle of an average city in Asia Minor winds down as twilight draws her blanket of stars across the landscape. Lykos, bronze worker of Thyatira, and quite proficient at his job, looked approvingly at his workmanship. Having mastered the art of mixing in just the right amount of tin, Lykos' work was perfect for the current heavy demand for cymbals. Lykos grunted with approval—this month he would feed his family, afford a new robe for his wife, and continue to provide for the poor within his church.

The sound of a *caliga*, a Roman boot, echoed on the stone street outside his shop. Ahenobarbus, old "Bronze Beard" himself, the chief of Lykos' guild, limped in, still bearing the consequences of his wound from his days in the Roman army. Though hardly an actual Roman, neither did Ahenobarbus hail locally from Asia Minor; nevertheless, he had acclimated well to the local culture, embracing all there was to embrace (quite often literally!).

"Remember, Lykos, the guild feast is coming up! Your presence is required this time. Apollo deserves your gratitude, and it's about time you feasted and drank with your comrades, don't you think?" Noticing Lykos' troubled complexion, Ahenobarbus fixed him with a piercing stare. "Is there a problem?"

Lykos felt as if one of his own workshop's bronze weights had sunk deep into the pit of his stomach. "*Problem*"? When the feast itself fixated on a pagan god, whom they called the "Son of Zeus," when Lykos himself was pledged to Jesus, the true Son of God? "*Problem*"? When the guild-master himself took every opportunity to brag about his "exploits" at these feasts, exploits involving sacred (and not-so-sacred) prostitutes or anybody else willing to get within arms-reach of him? "*Problem*"? When the amount of drunkenness that went on was enough to make Bacchus himself blush?

True, just last week a very articulate woman in the church, who called herself a prophetess, had declared that participating in such feasts was not really such a big deal. It was all for the "civic good." Still, Lykos had an uneasy feeling about what the Apostles, or even Jesus Himself, might have to say about that …

The Background of Thyatira

Compared to her six sister cities mentioned in Revelation, everything about Thyatira screams "average" … with one exception (as we shall see). Located at the site of the modern city of Akhisar, Thyatira gives us very little archaeological or inscriptional data to proclaim her uniqueness. Consequently, Hemer can proclaim that she is the "least known, least important and least remarkable of the cities."[1] Conquered by Rome in 190 BC, Thyatria was located between Pergamum and Sardis, southeast of the former by approximately forty miles. Although she could boast of having had a significant military presence as far back as 200 years ago,[2] and though she was hardly an "ugly duckling" compared to her sisters, Thyatira was simply "average" to any routine visitor.

Yet for those who had settled down and actually lived there, one social construct would stand out: the guilds. As in any society in any age, often artisans and vendors of like ilk would form associations, even while competing with each other. That way, when something (or *someone*, as we see in Acts 19:24–29) threatened their collective livelihood, action could be taken and disaster avoided. In the process, even while competing with each other, fellow craftsman could form social bonds that would last a lifetime. After all, a friend who is quite conversant with your livelihood is certainly

---

1 Hemer, *Letters to the Seven Churches of Asia Minor*, 106.
2 Osborne, *Revelation*, 151.

better than a friend who does not know the difference between bronze and gold!

Many cities had guilds, and generally each guild had its own god or goddess, like a divine mascot which was supposed to bless the endeavors of the craftsmen and artisans. In light of that, the guild feasts naturally possessed a strong religious aura, with the god or goddess as the center of attention. Failing to attend the feasts, especially due to ideological convictions, would have potentially serious economic repercussions.[1] As we have seen already in previous chapters, one could worship any god they wished but they were *expected* to worship particular gods and goddesses (local divine patrons) to "demonstrate social solidarity."[2]

However, in Thyatira the guilds played a much more dominant role than in the other cities (like college basketball in North Carolina compared to, say, Wyoming). Furthermore, Apollo Tyrimnaeus, who was heralded as the "son of Zeus," seems to have been explicitly connected with the trade guilds here in Thyatira. Clearly, then, any Christian who was himself a craftsman faced a dilemma when it came time to honor Apollo: "Whenever Christians refused to participate in the feasts because such participation would compromise their faith, they faced the anger of the pagan populace, and it had economic repercussions if they lost their jobs."[3] Indeed, in an era where religion is a "private" matter, it is hard for us to remember that for most of history religion functioned within a social matrix. Within the layers of society, from the Roman Empire down to the local village and even your own family, nobody cared *who* you worshipped, as long as you gave due reverence with the rest of your peers to the proper god, goddess, or Emperor. It was not *who* you worshipped but rather who you *neglected* to worship that mattered. Failure to worship the appropriate gods, goddesses, and demi-gods (like the emperor) meant more than "you're not a team player"; it meant you were actively courting disaster on behalf of your social

---

1 Ibid., 151–152.
2 Hurtado, "The Distinctiveness of Early Christianity," n.p.
3 Osborne, *Revelation*, 157.

group. The next flood, drought, or earthquake could be placed at the foot of the Christian who did not honor Apollo with the rest of the guild.

Jesus' Message to Thyatira

The church at Thyatira represents the complete 180° opposite of Ephesus, where we started. In fact, Jesus deliberately contrasts the two, as indicated by the fact that the noun "love" (*agape*) only occurs in Revelation 2:4 and 2:19, and Jesus makes it a point to emphasize Thyatira's "works"; whereas Ephesus needed to repent and perform her "first works," Thyatira could declare that her "later works" were even greater than her "first works."[1] For Thyatira, "The quality of life in this church was not diminishing. They were continuing to grow in their good deeds, ... There were more good deeds and they had more impact than when Thyatira was a young church. This is high praise indeed."[2]

Yet on the other hand, whereas Ephesus was zealous for correct theology, Thyatira had experienced some significant lapses in this regard. So Ephesus was strong in doctrine but weak in "love" and "good works"; Thyatira was strong in "love" and "good works" (and getting stronger) but weak in doctrine. Jesus continues to demonstrate that churches with a "one-track mind," whether it be for theology or for praxis, may still fall short. Both ortho*doxy* (believing what is right) and ortho*praxy* (doing what is right, especially works of love), are essential to avoid judgment.

Significantly, Thyatira is the only church that is actually praised for her love.[3] In retrospect, this should cause us to pause and do some soul-searching: if, out of seven of the earliest churches of Asia Minor, only one of them was known for "love," could it be that practicing love is actually harder than one would think? In other words, do we automatically take it for granted that "because we're

---

1 Walvoord, *Revelation of Jesus Christ*, 73.
2 Osborne, *Revelation*, 154–155.
3 Walvoord, *Revelation of Jesus Christ*, 73.

a Christian church, that means we love each other" when in reality we may be lacking the very thing we take for granted?

In 2:18, Jesus introduces himself as the one whose eyes are "like unto a flame of fire" and whose feet resemble "fine brass" (KJV; the NIV has "like burnished bronze"). This, like Revelation 1:14–15, hearken back to Daniel 10:6, demonstrating continuity between John's visions and Daniel's visions. However, the particular word used for "fine brass" is an extremely rare and difficult word, most likely referring to "a high-quality metal alloy of the copper, bronze, or brass type" and also alluding "to the important local guild of bronze workers."[1] Jesus is letting the church know that he is both fully aware of the dilemma they face with the guilds and that he, ultimately, is to be feared more than anybody or anything in the city. Similarly, later on (verse 23) Jesus will remind the church that he is the one who tests their innermost being (literally, "the kidneys and hearts," drawing from Jeremiah 17:10.[2] He sees all, and, more than anybody else, he is the judge they should be concerned about.

The letter to Thyatira is surprisingly the only one of the seven letters, in fact the only place in Revelation, where Jesus is called "the Son of God." The reason is two-fold. First, Jesus needs to remind his audience that, in contrast to Apollo, the "son of Zeus," Jesus is the true "Son of God."[3] While all believers, to a certain degree, may be called "God's sons" or "God's daughters," the Messiah reserves for himself the designation "*the* Son" (cf. John 20:31; 1 John 5:5; etc.) The relationship which Jesus has with the Father is unparalleled in the entire universe. Secondly, in Revelation 2:26–27, Jesus will reference Psalm 2, and within that Psalm we have a clear reference to "the Son" (vv. 7 and 12).[4] Consequently, Jesus "brackets" (vv. 18 and 27) the majority of the letter with reference to Psalm 2, a psalm which depicts the triumph of the Davidic Messiah (God's "Son") over the pagan forces that absurdly believe they can oppose

---

1 Hemer, *Letters to the Seven Churches of Asia Minor*, 111, 116.
2 Ibid., 122.
3 Ibid., 116.
4 Witherington, *Revelation*, 104.

Israel's God. In the letter to Thyatira, then, Jesus desires to remind his audience of his own supremacy over any opposition they may encounter. The message remains the same for the church today: the idea that the political and social forces of the world can truly oppose the kingdom of Jesus Christ is laughable. They would do well to heed the warning to "kiss" (i.e., "pay reverence to," Psalm 2:12) the Son before it is too late.

As we have seen, the church at Thyatira has much to commend it. Unlike Ephesus, these believers demonstrate Jesus' love to each other, they serve, they have faith, and they endure in the midst of pressure. The quality of their good deeds is increasing. Whereas Ephesus forgot what it was like to show love (both to Jesus and to each other), the church at Thyatira keeps outdoing herself in love.[1]

Perhaps because of their tendency to "love," however, Thyatira has been avoiding a confrontation and thus allowing a cancer to fester within the body. Jesus specifically says that the church "permits" or "allows" Jezebel to both "teach" and "deceive" Jesus' own servants, encouraging both immorality and pagan meals.

This "Jezebel," most likely not her real name, seems to be teaching more-or-less what the Nicolaitans and those following "Balaam" in 2:14 taught. The problem, then, is not with the fact that she was claiming to be a prophetess *per se* (both the Old and the New Testament have plenty of legitimate "prophetesses," e.g., Judges 4:4; Luke 2:36; Acts 21:9). The problem was pagan syncretism. As noted in the previous chapter, the "banquets" of a city were a mixture of both paganism (worship and reverence of idols and/or the emperor) and licentiousness (an opportunity for casual sex). The official guild feasts of Thyatira would have been no different. In fact, the temptation would have been stronger, since financial as well as social consequences awaited the Christian who refused to attend; in addition, "The guilds themselves were devoted to

---

[1] As noted above, there seems to be a deliberate contrast going on here between Ephesus and Thyatira (see Walvoord, *Revelation of Jesus Christ*, 73).

Where Is Your Allegiance? 91

good works," adding another reason for a love-minded Christian to justify attending.[1]

In a sense, then, the problem is *not* that Jezebel and her followers were pagan to the core, with Christianity tacked on as an extra religion. Rather, the problem, as J. Nelson Kraybill aptly puts it, is that "Jezebel may simply have been a pragmatist." In other words, she was advocating participation in cultic rituals as simply a means of "surviving economically and socially."[2] The name "Jezebel" itself, as Allan McNicol points out, was held by "one of the most notorious syncretists in the history of Israel," and thus whoever this "prophetess" is, "instead of resisting the incipient syncretism emerging in the church at Thyatira, … [she] is encouraging it."[3]

Furthermore, Jezebel was probably marketing her teaching as that which would help Christians attain "the deeper things of God"; in other words, to be able to attend these guild feasts freely represented a higher form of spirituality.[4] "Come, enjoy the feasts," Jezebel beckoned, "be one of the 'cool' Christians!"

To this, Jesus derisively responds that her teaching is actually the "deep things of Satan" (2:24). Furthermore, Jesus seems to be making the point that Jezebel's teaching is contrary to the apostolic doctrine set forth at the Jerusalem council in Acts 15 (the Greek word for "burden" in Revelation 2:24, *baros*, is also used in Acts 15:28).[5] The expression "as they say" in verse 24 might belong to the following clause and thus refer to James and the apostolic

---

1 Hemer, *Letters to the Seven Churches of Asia Minor*, 123.
2 J. Nelson Kraybill, *Apocalypse and Allegiance* (Grand Rapids, MI: Brazos, 2010), 162.
3 McNicol, *Conversion of the Nations*, 107–108.
4 Witherington, *Revelation*, 104; Hemer, *Letters to the Seven Churches of Asia Minor*, 123.
5 See the discussion in Hemer, *Letters to the Seven Churches of Asia Minor*, 123. Hemer states, "I think the point is that membership necessarily involved contradiction of the Apostolic decree [Acts 15] and the needed repentance must necessarily involve repudiation of the guilds. Here, as at Ephesus and Pergamum, the Christian's hardest pressure came from the inducements to conform to paganism rather than Judaism."

council.[1] This would mean that Jesus is simultaneously reiterating the fact that Christians are not under the Torah, but also affirming, with James and the apostolic council in Acts 15:19–21, 28–29, that idolatrous association was out of the question for Gentile Christians.

Jesus, together with the very first Apostolic council (called together specifically to deal with the new covenant ethics of an increasingly Gentile church), draws a line in the sand over which no Christian can cross. Idolatry, in any form, under any circumstances, cannot be participated in; furthermore, any so-called Christian who encourages Christians that idolatrous feasts are "ok" will face a fiery and frightening confrontation with the true Son of God.

"Idolatry" should, of course, be defined. Unfortunately, a comprehensive examination of the concept is beyond the scope of this book (the reader who wishes to pursue such a study should begin with G. K. Beale's *We Become What We Worship: A Biblical Theology of Idolatry*).[2] I believe, however, we should take as our basic starting point both Martin Luther's statement that an idol is "whatever your heart clings to and relies on …; trust and faith of the heart alone make both God and idol" and J. A. Motyer's definition, "The idol is whatever claims the loyalty that belongs to God alone."[3]

Part of idolatry is, I believe, the concept of "reverence," by which I mean "the exaltation to the level of the supernatural." Thus, for example, to "revere" Caesar is to see him as exalted to the point that he is beyond mere mortals, divinely inspired for his task as "savior of the Cosmos" via the *pax Romana*. To "revere" one's ancestors by praying to them is imply either that they are worthy of reverence not due still-living human beings or that they are supernaturally capable of intervening in the affairs of humans. To revere a local god is to offer sacrifices or even obeisance to it in

---

1 Walvoord, *Revelation of Jesus Christ*, 76 (Walvoord is following the argument of Henry Alford here).
2 G. K. Beale, *We Become What We Worship: A Biblical Theology of Idolatry* (Downers Grove, IL: InterVarsity, 2008).
3 Both cited in Beale, *We Become What We Worship*, 17.

such a way that implies it is capable of supernaturally intervening (I say "implies"; one can offer reverence outwardly whether or not one truly believes the idol is a "god," yet this still publicly implies that one *does* believe it is a god).

Yet since the gods of this world are nothing compared to the one true God, and since Caesar himself is nothing more than any other "man," then for a Christian to reverence them creates a conflict of interest, for they have already pledged themselves to the one true God and His Son Jesus Christ. While the pagan gods (and Caesar) declare, "Have as many gods and goddesses as you want, but revere me too," the one true God declares, "Thou shalt have no other gods before me."

To ignore that commandment, then, and revere/worship anybody but the Triune God is deliberate rebellion. Such actions demonstrate that one is not truly giving the Lord Jesus Christ the allegiance he demands. Just as the words "forsaking all others" have traditionally been incorporated into wedding vows, so coming to Christ for salvation must, of necessity, imply those same words. Yet just as the one true God cannot tolerate rivals in the supernatural realm, so also his true Son cannot tolerate any rivals on earth, whether emperor, president, preacher, pop star, or athlete. The message of Revelation, as David DeSilva points out, is that we must take "the path to honor that way of life which refused to share the honor of God (or of God's Anointed) with another at any cost."[1] Jesus does not willingly share our allegiance with others.

The consequences for leading God's people astray in this regard are severe (Revelation 2:22–23). This "Jezebel" herself, since she ignored the opportunity to turn aside from her false teaching, will be punished harshly (the word for "bed" here quite often refers to a "sick bed," not merely a location of rest;[2] thus the NIV's "bed of suffering" is an appropriate translation). Those who have actually followed her teaching and have polluted themselves with idolatry

---

1 deSilva, "Honor Discourse and the Rhetorical Strategy of the Apocalypse of John," 89.
2 Osborne, *Revelation*, 159.

and immorality will be killed "with death," probably meaning "with a plague."[1] This perhaps echoes the Johannine concept of a "sin unto death" in 1 John 5:16 (notice the expression "his brother," apparently implying in this context that the person is a Christian). In other words, a point exists where Jesus himself may step in and remove a Christian who is harming his or her testimony.

The consequences are serious for the compromiser, yet for the Christian who overcomes, Jesus promises something incredible. Utilizing the Messianic language of Psalm 2, the Christian is promised "authority over the nations" and the ability to crush those in rebellion to God. The language is almost identical to the Septuagint (Greek) Psalm 2; the word "rule" (KJV and NIV) is, interestingly, the usual word for "shepherding" (*poimainō*) in the Greek, but occasionally can refer idiomatically to a violent striking (e.g., LXX Micah 5:6). In fact, the "rod of iron" referred to here is not the normal shepherd's crook, as in Psalm 23, but most likely "a large wooden club capped with iron for killing animals that endangered the sheep."[2] In other words, there is a world of difference between the gentle "shepherding" of Psalm 23 (the Lord with his children) and the violent "shepherding" of Psalm 2 (the Lord shattering his enemies).

We may cringe at the violence here in verse 27, but it cannot be overlooked. This multi-ethnic group of Overcomers, together with the Messiah, will shatter those nations that dare oppose Jesus. We no doubt see the ultimate culmination of this promise in Rev19:11–21, where the armies of heaven (probably not angels, since the members of this army are "clothed in white linen," cf. 19:8) accompany the Lamb in this epic conflict between Christ and Antichrist.

Truly God is Love, and John himself has earlier made that point clear. Yet a universe in rebellion cannot be permitted to remain so indefinitely; the rulers who dare raise their fists in rebellion against the Messiah (Psalm 2:1–3) have made a choice. It is them

---

1 Witherington, *Revelation*, 105.
2 Osborne, *Revelation*, 166–167.

and the Beast versus the Lamb—this can only result in the Lamb shattering them rather than shepherding them.

In this way, Jesus "frames" his message to Thyatira with references to Psalm 2 (vv. 18, 26–27). In doing so, he is in essence declaring that those who compromise are casting their lot in with the "rulers" and "heathen" of Psalm 2:1, exemplified in the coming antichrist of Revelation. In other words, there is no neutrality. One cannot claim allegiance to Jesus and offer reverence to pagan gods or human rulers. This is more than an academic issue: in many religions (e.g., the casual Buddhist-Shinto hybrid of most Japanese, sprinkled liberally with ancestor worship), a man or woman may be willing to acknowledge Jesus as worthy of worship along with other gods, one's ancestors, etc. Yet to declare that Jesus is worthy of worship *to the exclusion of all others* requires a radical step of faith. In other words, there is no more "hedging the bets." One must commit all-or-nothing to Jesus Christ, even at the expense of one's economic livelihood. To commit oneself to Jesus means that there is no "plan B," no "second-stringer" like Buddha or an ancestor to substitute in when Jesus does not work out. It is all or nothing.

We have one final promise given to the overcomers in Thyatira: Jesus will give them "the morning star." Frankly, nobody is sure what this means. However, Ben Witherington's guess is as good as any, namely that "The morning star is Venus, which to the Romans was the symbol of victory and sovereignty. Christians will not obtain such things through pagan rituals or by following pagan teaching, but from Christ."[1]

In an era where many people attempt to attain "victory" in their life through influence, prestige, material possessions, and enough "self-help" books to sink a battleship, this fact is worth remembering: allegiance to Jesus Christ is what truly brings victory.

---

1 Witherington, *Revelation*, 105.

QUESTIONS FOR FURTHER DISCUSSION

1. What sets Jezebel apart from the good prophetesses in the Old and New Testament?
2. In what ways is it easy for a sparkling personality to lure us into sin? How can we guard against this?
3. What are some ways, even in modern society, that "worship" of Jesus Christ is inappropriately combined with reverence for other things?

SARDIS—
THE VULNERABLE
FORTRESS

As if taken straight from an epic battle scene, the fortress of Sardis was majestically situated above the city below; on three sides, a sheer cliff plummeted down 1500 feet. On the fourth side, the citadel was accessible, but just barely—a "narrow saddle" linked to the "ridge of Tmolus," yet this connection was itself "steep and difficult."[1] Needless to say, in an era before gunpowder, such a fortress could withstand any siege so long as food and water lasted. Indeed, even during the time Revelation was written, the expression "to capture the acropolis of Sardis" meant "to do the impossible."[2] Only a fool would attempt to take this city!

And yet not once but twice in her history, Sardis *had* been taken, and both times as "a thief in the night." Her walls were secure enough, but the soldiers manning them were not. Lack of vigilance, not structural weakness, led to her downfall. When, in his foolishness, the mighty king Croesus thought he could resist the inevitable and defeat the Persian empire, he was eventually forced to retreat to his massive citadel (not having realized that the Persians were more than willing to launch a sneak attack in winter). Safe and secure in this castle, Croesus little realized that one of his enemies' soldiers had managed to find a way up the cliffs, into the fortress, and to the gates.

Centuries later, Sardis was one again besieged by a king with imperial ambitions, Antiochus III. In this case, as described in chapter 1, Lagoras led an elite team up the cliffs, securing the gates

---

1 Hemer, *Letters to the Seven Churches of Asia Minor*, 129.
2 Ibid., 133.

so that the army could enter in. Once again, lack of vigilance caused the capture of the fortress. To the church in the city sitting under the shadow of that same fortress, Jesus orders them, "Be alert!"

THE BACKGROUND OF SARDIS

Rich, powerful, breathtaking, and historically relevant—Sardis could claim all of these descriptions, or, rather, she *used to be able to*, once upon a time. Sardis was, indeed, "living on past historical prestige."[1]

First of all, Sardis could boast that she had been visited by none other than Midas of Phrygia, who, according to legend, washed off his "golden touch" in the "springs of Pactolus." Indeed, that gold dust could be found in those springs was undisputed historically, and ancient records all agree that Sardis had plenty of gold to spare.[2] According to legend, Sardis was the first to mint coinage. Undisputed, however, is the fact that Sardis, like Laodicea, gained much wealth from its textiles, dyes, and jewelry to add to its already significant pile of gold.[3] When an earthquake hit both Sardis and Philadelphia in AD 17, it took only nine years for Sardis to be back on her feet, contesting with other Anatolian cities for the right to dedicate a temple to the emperor.[4]

Historically, Sardis predated the Persian empire. While Babylon still reigned supreme in the Middle East, and the Medes still dominated the Persians, King Gyges developed a significantly wealthy kingdom in Asia Minor based in Sardis, a dynasty that would culminate in Croesus who tried bravely (though unsuccessfully) to halt the expansion of Cyrus the Great one hundred years later.[5] The continued importance of Sardis is attested by the fact that the local governor of this region of the Persian Empire utilized

---

1 Witherington, *Revelation*, 105.
2 Hemer, *Letters to the Seven Churches of Asia Minor*, 130–131.
3 Walvoord, *Revelation of Jesus Christ*, 78.
4 Ibid., 134.
5 Ibid., 131.

Sardis as the seat of his authority, despite (or perhaps because of) its location far west in the proximity of Greece.

As far as religion goes, Zeus Lydios (a "customized" Zeus for the Lydians), Heracles, and Dionysus all seem to have been prominent in Sardis. In addition, a variation of Artemis/Ephesus, "Cybele," was revered, and as "protectress of the city" was portrayed as having "a turreted headdress" in addition to "ears and stalks of corn, a poppy flower or head, two lighted torches, and coiled serpents," often depicted as "travelling in a car [carriage] drawn by two winged serpents."[1]

What was unique about Sardis, however, is that the populace seems to have been a bit more obsessed than usual with mystery cults.[2] Prominent among these was the mystery religion of Cybele and Attis: both were "guardians of the grave, and the after-life was originally seen as a reunion with the Earth-Mother. The serpents associated with the goddess were seen to emerge from the earth and possessed the power of rejuvenation by sloughing their skins."[3]

The Cyble and Attis myth, as it existed in the 1st century, was predictably bizarre and tragic. While variations exist, the gist of the story is that Cybele, the goddess, had a consort, the shepherd Attis. Angry at Attis, the goddess drove him insane, causing Attis to castrate himself, dying. The goddess attempted to reanimate him but, instead of an actual resurrection, managed merely to preserve his body with the added bonus that his hair would grow and his little finger would move (no evidence exists for any concept of a truly "resurrected" Attis until the 2nd century AD, long after Christianity had been established and proliferated).[4] Nevertheless, the concept of a "life-and-death-and-rejuvenation" cycle, as encoded in some form in Cybele herself (more so than Attis), played a prominent role in this mystery religion (and others) celebrated in Sardis.

---

1 Ibid., 138–139.
2 Walvoord, *Revelation of Jesus Christ*, 78.
3 Hemer, *Letters to the Seven Churches of Asia Minor*, 139.
4 J. Ed Komoszewski, M. James Sawyer, and Daniel B. Wallace, *Reinventing Jesus* (Grand Rapids, MI: Kregel, 2006), 252–254.

To summarize, then, Sardis possessed the best historical reputation for power and riches (since she was both an impenetrable fortress and the beneficiary of the "Midas touch") in Asia Minor and was obsessed with life and death. Significantly, Jesus will declare that her church is more dead than alive, and needs to regain her vigilance rather than basking comfortably in the shadow of her reputation.

JESUS' MESSAGE TO SARDIS

Jesus' opening statement, "the one holding the seven Spirits of God and the seven stars," offers both warning and hope. The reference to the "seven Spirits," as we have seen, is somewhat difficult; Osborne and Hemer see it as alluding to Zechariah 4:2, 10, while Walvoord sees a connection to Isaiah 11:2 (though this does not necessarily have to be an "either-or" situation).[1] Regardless, the fact that Jesus "owns" both the seven-fold Spirit of God and the churches to which he is speaking demonstrates his authority over the entire situation. Fortunately, however, Jesus' possession of the Spirit "details the complete and adequate work of the Spirit in the community. The church of Sardis, nearly dead (3:1–2), can be revived only if the Spirit takes over."[2] The fact that Jesus urges the church essentially to "wake up" in v. 2 indicates "that there was a flicker that could be rekindled."[3]

What, then, was the problem with Sardis? Interestingly, of all the seven churches, Sardis is addressed in the least context-specific terms. In other words, we don't know what was going on except the general condemnations Jesus levels against them: their reputation for being alive is false (v. 1), they are not diligent (2), their deeds have failed to impress (2), they have fallen and need to get back up (3), and only a small minority of them have not "soiled their garments" (4). We do not know if Sardis suffered from the

---

1 See Osborne, *Revelation*, 173; Hemer, *Letters to the Seven Churches of Asia Minor*, 142; Walvoord, *Revelation of Jesus Christ*, 79.
2 Osborne, *Revelation*, 173.
3 Witherington, *Revelation*, 105.

Where Is Your Allegiance? 101

pagan syncretism of Pergamum or the lack of love of Ephesus. Fortunately, though, since Jesus does not threaten them with either warfare or extinction like those two, Sardis' problem may have been a more general spiritual sloppiness, less severe than Ephesus and Pergamum, yet all-pervasive nonetheless. Jesus, after all, does not have anything good to say about them. Sardis may not have been the spectacularly dismal 2015–16 Philadelphia 76ers, which managed to set a record for the worst losing streak in US sports. Rather, Sardis is more like the 2015–16 Washington Wizards—not horrific, but just mediocre enough to miss the playoffs.

The reason for this church's failure, as Jesus makes clear, is lack of vigilance (like the fortress' own guards). Content in their own reputation and their own sense of security, the church, like the fortress, has let little sins slip in unnoticed, sins which threaten to open up the gates to a shipwrecked conscience. Thus Jesus commands them to "be vigilant" (KJV "be watchful"; NIV "wake up!") in verse 2. The consequences of failing to "wake up" is that Jesus himself will be forced to show up unannounced, like a "thief in the night."

Jesus' rebuke here is linked to the concept of one's "name." In this message to Sardis, Jesus places a lot of emphasis on "name" (Greek *onoma*), a word which means "reputation," "person," and "status" in 3:1, 4, and 5, respectively. Sardis' "name" (i.e., "reputation") was that they were alive and vibrant. Jesus corrects this misconception, declaring that their name is "death." In light of the local pagan obsession with life-and-death cycles, Osborne notes the "irony" of Sardis, that "they claim the Christian 'name,' 'Life,' but actually retain the pagan name, 'Death.' It is a sad thing when the only accomplishment ('deed') of a church is what it names itself, …"[1]

Fortunately, there are a few names in this church who "have not defiled their garments" (v. 4). This apt imagery resonates nicely with the background of the textile industry in Sardis: "The soiled garment in a city famous for its dyed garments and fancy clothing

---

1 Osborne, *Revelation*, 173–174.

products would be antithetical to civic pride."[1] This minority of believers, then, represents the true potential of the church while the others fall short of her reputation. These names will have their "names" in the book of life and their names will be confessed by Jesus himself before the Father and the angels.

The significance of this statement cannot be overlooked: to confess a name is to grant it validity, importance, and Revelation as a whole offers us a sharp dichotomy of those names associated with Jesus versus those associated with the Beast. In other words, the status of your "name" reveals your allegiance. Some names in Revelation will swear allegiance to the Beast by bearing the Beast's name (Revelation 14:11, "The mark of his name ..."; cf. 13:17). These stand in opposition to the Lamb, because one cannot identify with both Jesus and the Beast; the latter, who has a "name of blasphemy," stands in opposition to the Lamb's "name" (13:1, 6). Furthermore, those who bear the name of the Beast do not have their names written in the Lamb's book of life, and consequently will face destruction (13:8, 14:11). In contrast, those names who have the Lamb's name on their foreheads (Revelation 22:4) have their own name written in the book of life, glorify the Father's name (Revelation 15:4), and thus gain victory over the Beast's "name" (Revelation 15:2—"and over the number of his name").

Consequently, a strong connection exists between whose "name" we bear and whether or not our own names are written in the Lamb's Book of Life. In addition, whether or not one's name is written in the Book of Life seems to be inextricably linked to one's status as an "overcomer." As discussed before, the "overcomer" in Revelation is the one who has pledged allegiance to the Lamb rather than the Beast, and thus overcomes because of the power of the Lamb. The act of "overcoming" is generated from the power of the blood of the Lamb (12:11); i.e., this is the *cause* of the Christian's victory. However, neither can we escape the conclusion that "overcoming" is somehow closely connected with deeds (see 2:26, and the message to Thyatira). The implication of 3:2, 5 is not that

---

1 Witherington, *Revelation*, 106.

the works of the church in Sardis are insufficient to save them, but rather that their works are insufficient to identify them as a "overcomers." The solution for the majority, to regain their reputation ("name") as "overcomers" like the minority, is to "strengthen what remains," where "what remains" seems to indicate the spiritual minority, which was itself in danger of dying out.[1] Also, though five out of the seven of the churches are urged to repent, significantly only Ephesus and Sardis are called to "remember" before "repenting" (2:5 and 3:3).[2]

In other words, most of the believers in Sardis have lost their reputation of being "overcomers." The solution is to "strengthen" those few faithful ones that are still obviously "overcomers" by paying more attention to them and allowing them to lead the church. The best cure for a lazy sentry is to pair him with a diligent sentry—professing Christians who have come to realize their own spiritual sluggishness should look to mature, spiritually alert men and women. The result will be confident group of Christians who throw off their sluggishness and diligently persevere in their testimony (cf. Hebrews 6:11–12).

The question confronting Sardis and many churches today, then, is this: will they regain their "name" as "the victorious ones," a name that they have lost, collectively, through lack of spiritual diligence? One's "name" here is not, of course, external reputation (e.g., "Church X is a really cool place because they have an espresso bar!"), but rather its value in the kingdom of God, its loyalty to Jesus Christ. Many a church which originally trumpeted the Gospel, proclaimed the praises of the King with a pure heart, and lived out God's plan through love towards others has slowly but surely lost its effectiveness and usefulness because it did not alertly guard against the temptations of pride, arrogance, hateful anger, etc. Satisfaction with one's reputation and outward status—such is the great stumbling block that threatens to trip up churches like that at Sardis.

---

1 Osborne, *Revelation*, 175.
2 Hemer, *Letters to the Seven Churches of Asia Minor*, 144–5.

The athlete involved in pre-season training and the marine recruit at Parris Island forced to produce a seeming infinity of pushups, if truly committed, do not consider the difficulties they are currently undergoing, nor do they stop to consider whether or not their current "status" is sufficient. Rather, for the glory of what awaits, they persevere. In the same way, the church at Sardis is called to consider the glory that awaits if they are proven worthy (3:4): the privilege of marching with the King of Kings in an imperial triumph procession ("they will walk with me in white garments"). Traditionally, after a Roman victory, the "conqueror walking in his triumphal procession" would be accompanied by "white-clad attendants."[1] Those companions of the conqueror bask in the glory of the victorious one. The final choice awaiting the church at Sardis, then, is this: slack off and be invaded and judged by the very Conqueror you've pledged allegiance to, or regain your vigilance, reclaim your reputation, and join the victorious procession of the Lamb.

QUESTIONS FOR FURTHER DISCUSSION

1. What are some ways Christians today can become vulnerable to a lackadaisical attitude? (Think especially of how this might vary from culture to culture).
2. How can Christians remain vigilant in their faith in order to avoid spiritual laxness?

---

[1] Hemer, *Letters to the Seven Churches of Asia Minor*, 147; Osborne, *Revelation*, 179.

9. Philadelphia— Longing for a City with no Earthquakes

I magine the following scenario: you are sitting quietly at the kitchen table, deeply immersed in a book, when the toaster starts shaking, barely noticeable at first, but within seconds loudly rattling and threatening to fall off the counter. This is not a sign of the demonic possession of your favorite kitchen appliance, but rather (if you lived in Yokohama, Japan, like I did), the signal that an earthquake has arrived.

Philadelphia, like much of Japan, was essentially "earthquake city," so much so that Caesar himself, after the great quake of AD 17, granted them a hiatus from paying tribute. The average Christian of Philadelphia knew what it was like to be shaken up, to have to flee in terror outdoors for fear of being buried under the rubble of ancient history's fragile buildings.[1] In a sense, the earthquakes they constantly feared dovetailed with the persecution they were experiencing. Yet the King of Kings offers a special promise to this group of believers who faithfully endured both persecutions and earthquakes: They will never more have to flee outside.

The Background of Philadelphia

As anybody who has lived in Philadelphia, Pennsylvania knows, simply having your city named "Brotherly-Love" (*philei*,

---

1 See Hemer, *Letters to the Seven Churches of Asia Minor*, 156-7, for a discussion of the natural connection between earthquakes and fleeing outdoors.

"love" + *adelphos*, "brother") does not guarantee peace and tranquility. I have experienced both a Philadelphia traffic jam and a Phillies ballgame, and can thus attest that the city's reputation for "brotherly love" is highly overrated (though her fabulous cheese-steaks make up for it). In the case of Philadelphia, Asia Minor, however, the story behind the name is quite appropriate. Her founder, Attalus, was known for his love and devotion to his brother, the Greek king Eumenes, and vice versa. In fact, when Attalus heard a rumor of his brother's death and took over his position as king, Eumenes (whose demise was greatly exaggerated) returned yet forgave Attalus while the latter cheerfully returned to his position as second-in-command. Later, when rumors were flying around that Eumenes was consorting with the enemy Perseus, Rome offered Attalus assistance in taking over his brother's position, yet Attalus refused (only becoming king years later upon his brother's death).[1] The original "Philadelphia," then, was well-named.

Geographically, Philadelphia (now covered by the modern city of Alasehir) was situated on a major trade route from Smyrna to Lydia and Phrygia.[2] Furthermore, Philadelphia "lay on the major Roman postal road from Troas through Pergamum, Sardis, and then Philadelphia to the east. Thus the city was ideal for commerce and was called 'the gateway to the east.'"[3]

Yet Philadelphia also served as a different type of gateway—a cultural one. As "a city dedicated to Hellenistic culture" (in fact, years later it would be called "Little Athens"),[4] she ultimately functioned as "a missionary city" whose "purpose" was to "educate the peoples of newly annexed Lydia and Phrygia in Greek culture and loyalty to a Hellenized monarchy."[5] In other words, this was a city expected to have great influence, great cultural "power."

---

1 Hemer, *Letters to the Seven Churches of Asia Minor*, 155.
2 Osborne, *Revelation*, 184; Hemer, *Letters to the Seven Churches of Asia Minor*, 154–5.
3 Osborne, *Revelation*, 184.
4 Witherington, *Revelation*, 106.
5 Hemer, *Letters to the Seven Churches of Asia Minor*, 154–5. Regarding this point, Hemer interacts heavily with William Ramsay's work here, arguing

Philadelphia also benefited from extremely fertile volcanic soil in the region, suitable for growing grape vines. Significantly, her patron deity was Bacchus, the Greek god of wine.[1] The downside to her location was the incredible amount of earthquake activity, noted by ancient authors, especially the massive quake of AD 17 which seriously harmed both her and Sardis. This earthquake was so bad that Caesar withdrew his demand for tribute for five years, resulting in an immense feeling of affection for the emperor, affection which found its way into the coinage and, temporarily, the name "Neocaesarea."[2]

Such affection did not last long, however. In AD 92, shortly before Revelation was written, Domitian (probably desiring to facilitate the growing of corn to feed his troops), decreed that half of the vineyards in Asia Minor would be eliminated. Philadelphia, with Bacchus as her patron, would have been harmed more than most. Predictably, the citizens of Philadelphia may have experienced a "final disillusionment" with this imperial dynasty.[3]

JESUS' MESSAGE TO PHILADELPHIA

Jesus' self-designation in 3:7 begins predictably enough ("the holy One, the true One") before taking an odd twist, "the one having the keys of David." This puzzling phrase is slightly clarified by the following statement of Jesus' sovereignty: when Jesus opens a door, nobody can shut it, and when he closes a door, nobody can open it. This power and authority form the basis for the assurance that he has, in fact, "opened a door" for this church.

So what, exactly, does it mean to say that Jesus has the "keys of David"? First of all, this expression dovetails nicely with Jesus'

---

    that though Ramsay's "view is overstated, ... its general probability is consistent with the historical and geographical facts and with the methods of Attalid policy" (155).
1 Witherington, *Revelation*, 106.
2 Hemer, *Letters to the Seven Churches of Asia Minor*, 156–7.
3 Ibid., 158. Hemer also suggests that Revelation 6:6 may be an allusion to this event.

declaration in 1:20 that he "has the keys of hell and death," indicating his authority and triumph over both, his sovereign control. Naturally here in 3:7 the point is not "authority over David," but rather "the sort of authority that David would have." Consequently, Jesus is asserting his power as the Messianic (Davidic) King over all the earth, which means he also decides who is allowed into the Messianic kingdom (and Davidic kingdom, cf. 2 Samuel 7:16) and who is excluded from it.

Secondly, scholars recognize a strong similarity between this passage and Isaiah 22:20–25. The second half of Isaiah 22, interestingly, deals with a specific oracle against the royal treasurer, Shebna. Due to the fact that Shebna has been exalting himself (v. 16), the Lord will send Shebna into captivity, apparently into Assyria. In return, the godly Eliakim will receive the "key of the house of David" so that he can "open, and no one shut" and "shut, and no one will open."[1] Eliakim, in a sense, stands as "a type of the exalted Christ who controls 'the keys of the kingdom.'"[2]

Philadelphia is a church that needs to be reminded and encouraged by the fact that Jesus Christ alone administers the entrance into the Kingdom. We see the reason for this in 3:9—Jesus' own ethnic kinsman, who should have accepted the Messiah, have not only rejected him but also rejected his followers. Most likely Jewish and Gentile Christians were being excluded from the synagogue, and thus denied the opportunity to publicly worship the one true God in the most obvious place. Thus Jesus felt it necessary to remind them of his ultimate authority to determine who, in reality, belongs in the community of faith.[3]

---

1 Peter A. Steveson, *A Commentary on Isaiah* (Greenville, SC: BJU Press, 2003), 183–185. Significantly, as Steveson points out, even Eliakim is not guaranteed this permanent position, since vv. 24–25 demonstrate "the inevitable result of nepotism" if Eliakim "lets his relatives take advantage of his position."
2 Osborne, *Revelation*, 187.
3 Hemer, *Letters to the Seven Churches in Asia Minor*, 161; Osborne, *Revelation*, 188. I would, however, caution us from seeing this as a straightforward "Jew vs. Gentile" confrontation in Philadelphia. Surely

Perhaps due to their being denied access to the synagogue, the church at Philadelphia was, to all outward appearances, insignificant (v. 8, "you have a little strength"). This is not a criticism,[1] but rather an ironic statement—"In the eyes of the world (and the local synagogue), you are insignificant, but as far as I'm concerned you have kept my word and not denied my name, even under pressure, so I am giving you an 'open door.'"

The theological significance of this commendation cannot be overlooked, and should be a cause of rejoicing for small churches everywhere, so long as Jesus owns their allegiance. Size, influence, and public perception are *not* the ultimate determiners of a church's worth in the eyes of God. What matters is whether or not a church yields itself wholly to Jesus Christ (evidenced by keeping his word and not denying his name). Such a church may experience slower growth than others which compromise (consider Sardis, for example, which had a "name" [i.e., "reputation"] that it was alive, but was actually dead); such a church may be mocked and ridiculed by those around it; such a church may occasionally despair of making any significant difference in their community. In a great North American city, some "mega-churches" may draw crowds with a watered-down Gospel or a less-confrontational Jesus, while the house church in China or a small church in India lives under the constant pressure of ridicule (at best) or physical violence (at worst). Yet in the eyes of Jesus Christ, such a church is precious and may yet see greater opportunities to expand the kingdom as a result of her faithfulness. It is "faithfulness," not "success" which "has always been the test of divine blessing."[2] The church that feels they have reached "success" simply because of their large numbers needs to take a closer look at themselves.

So what, exactly, is this "open door" of v. 8? In keeping with the theme of Jesus' sovereignty over the Kingdom, and in light of

---

    even by this time the church still contained a significant percentage of Jewish believers, even in Asia Minor.
1 See Osborne, *Revelation*, 189, for why this is most likely not a criticism.
2 Ibid.

this church's unfailing allegiance to him, we should probably take it to mean, first of all, the "open door to the Kingdom of heaven."[1] This fits with the consistent theme of "overcomers" in Revelation (e.g., for example, Revelation 21:7, where the one overcoming will inherit either "all things" or "this" [the water of life?], depending on one's translation).

Nevertheless, the "open door" language does naturally lend itself to the concept of "opportunity," i.e., the opportunity for missionary activity. The Apostle Paul used the same language in 2 Corinthians 2:12. This is not an "either-or" situation. The expression may be deliberately ambiguous so that it can refer to multiple things, and perhaps both entrance into Jesus' kingdom and evangelistic opportunity are in view.[2] While the world regards this church as insignificant, the "door" that Jesus has "opened" for them signifies both their special access to the Father's Kingdom and their ability to exert divine influence on those around them.

This, then, is the result of allegiance: both the inheritance of the Kingdom and the opportunity to spread it. Such a church as Philadelphia, no matter how small, wields influence disproportionate to its size and will ultimately supplant all pretenders. They themselves go through the "open door" while also holding it open for others. Such a church, wherever it may be, can rest assured that while other, larger churches draw crowds for entertainment or for a "warm and fuzzy feeling," reaping temporary rewards, a church like Philadelphia can make a significant impact for the cause of Christ only measurable in eternity.

Hand-in-hand with the promise of an "open door" is Jesus' declaration of a great reversal in v. 9. Those who had mocked them will be forced to honor them. Interestingly, Jesus has taken an Old Testament prophecy referring to Israel's subjugation of the Gentiles from Isaiah 60:11–16. In this passage Israel is depicted as basically enjoying both honor from the Gentiles (a great reversal from their previous situation, see verse 15) and essentially enjoying the riches

---

1 Ibid., 188.
2 Hemer, *The Letters to the Seven Churches of Asia Minor*, 162.

Where Is Your Allegiance?

of the Gentiles (v. 16). This great reversal of Israel's fortunes will make it even more clear to them the status of the Lord as their Savior and Redeemer.

Yet Jesus, incredibly, takes this promise for Israel and also applies it to the Gentiles *at Israel's expense* (Revelation 3:9b seems to be an allusion to Isaiah 60:14 and the surrounding context).[1] Indeed, those of the synagogue ("of Satan") who had "locked the door," so to speak, will be forced to come and bow before Gentile believers (and Jewish believers as well), acknowledging that God has favored them above themselves. We see here, then, a parallel to the theme of Romans 11:11–26, in that Israel will be provoked to jealousy (vv. 11, 14), forced to acknowledge God's blessing of the Gentiles, yet this will ultimately result in their salvation. Jesus, like Paul, ultimately makes the point that ethnicity, or whether or not one still possesses a foreskin, or how well one keeps the Torah, makes not a whit of difference in one's spiritual standing before God. Allegiance to Jesus Christ, first and foremost, determines one's standing, and, as Revelation 3:9a indicates, anybody who claims to belong to the people of God yet stands in opposition to Jesus' claim as the Son of David, the Messianic king, is a liar.

As a result of this "great reversal," Jesus makes a very odd promise in Revelation 3:10. Although I prefer not to delve into eschatology in this book, nevertheless this verse is something of an anomaly and must be discussed. On the one hand, the syntax of the verse ("keep you from" [using the Greek word *ek*]) would seem to lend itself to the idea of a pretribulational rapture (the idea that the church will be "raptured away" before the 7-year time of tribulation begins), since "kept from the time of trouble" is the more likely reading than "kept *through* the time of trouble."[2] On the other

---

[1] See Hemer, *The Letters to the Seven Churches of Asia Minor*, 160–1, 163; Osborne, *Revelation*, 191.

[2] See, for example, the use of the preposition *ek* in such passages as Jn 10:39. However, the language would also allow for the concept of "rescued from out of the midst of," as seen in the use of *ek* in such passages as Jn 12:9. Finally, one may very well argue that the language could imply "kept safe from the effects of …" (John 12:27, perhaps?).

hand, this promise is apparently unique to Philadelphia based on their faithfulness, as compared to the other churches (regardless of spiritual status). It is difficult to take a promise given to a specific church, in contrast to other churches, and extrapolate it to refer to all true churches existing at the time of the rapture (after all, the promise would then ring hollow if, ironically, no churches existed in Alasehir at the rapture).

The better explanation, regardless of one's eschatological position, would seem to refer to a general time of persecution throughout the Empire, much closer in time to John's era than the Day of the Lord.[1] The concept of a pretribulational rapture may or may not be valid (and I would hold to the former position), yet I do not believe it can be proved from this verse. Regardless, in this passage we have the unique situation where lack of persecution is a sign of God's blessing, certainly not the norm in Scripture (cf. James 1:2).

Despite her prominent position in Revelation as being one of only two churches without rebuke, even Philadelphia is warned against slacking off in v. 11. The "crown" here represents "the athlete's crown of victory."[2] Jesus himself, having himself given them the crown, is the one who has the right to take it away.[3] The implication seems to be that rewards gained as a result of faithful allegiance can be lost through carelessness (and the church at Sardis has already demonstrated how easy it is to slack off spiritually).[4] Both Hemer and Osborne appropriately note the parallel to Romans 11:17–21.[5] Although the (predominantly) Gentile church

---

1 For a scholarly discussion on the issues of Revelation 3:10 by somebody who holds to a pretribulational rapture position, see chapter 8 (by Andrew M. Woods) in the book *Evidence for the Rapture: A Biblical Case for Pretribulationism*, ed. John F. Hart (Chicago: Moody, 2015).
2 Hemer, *Letters to the Seven Churches of Asia Minor*, 165.
3 Osborne, *Revelation*, 195.
4 I agree with Osborne, *Revelation*, 195, that "losing their rewards" seems to be what is in view here.
5 Osborne, *Revelation*, 195; Hemer, *Letters to the Seven Churches of Asia*, 165.

has risen to prominence in the Lord's plan for the world, nevertheless they should not boast themselves over the "natural branch" (Jews) lest they, too, be set aside: "The vacant room left by the lapse of a Church may be filled with the rise of another."[1]

Finally, to the true believer that overcomes, both Jew and Gentile, Jesus first offers the promise of becoming a "pillar in the temple" that no longer has to go outside, and, second, the promise of receiving three names. The significance of the former promise becomes all the more apparent when we consider the nature of Philadelphia as a city prone to earthquakes. Osborne states it best:

> ... [A]fter the earthquake of A.D. 17 much of the populace of the city was forced to move outside the city and take up residence on the farms. Jesus is promising that they will be secure in the city of God and will never again be dislodged from their homes. Now their lives are characterized by uncertainty and weakness ("little strength" in 3:8). Now they suffer physical harm (from the earthquakes) and external persecution. Then they would have the security and strength they long for.[2]

Furthermore, the theme of "earthquake" plays a role elsewhere in Revelation, during the tribulation, and is always cause for terror (Revelation 6:12; 8:5; 11:13, 19; 16:18). Yet to the very church that, possibly more than any other, would have known about earthquakes, Jesus says that they need no longer fear. They will be established as a mighty pillar in the New Jerusalem (which, as we see in 21:1–4, 22, essentially functions as the temple and at the same time replaces the temple), the ultimate City that will never suffer from earthquakes.

The significance of the "names" seems to derive first of all from Exodus 28:35–38, where the divine name itself appears on Aaron's forehead; secondly, the "new name" at the end of the verse

---

1   H. B. Swete, *The Apocalypse of St. John*, 2nd ed. (London: R&T Washbourne, 1907), cited in Hemer, *Letters to the Seven Churches of Asia*, 165.
2   Osborne, *Revelation*, 197.

may echo Isaiah 62:2, where the Jews are promised a "new name" from the mouth of the Lord himself.[1] We have already seen how much this particular letter draws from Isaiah, and this would be another way Jesus is emphasizing a "great reversal," that the Gentiles who had not known God are now given blessings formerly reserved strictly for the Jews (cf. 1 Peter 2:9–10). Each believer, then, "instead of being a pillar of pagan society," will actually be transformed into "a pillar in God's temple, with the most crucial of all things inscribed ... God's name, Jesus' name, and the name of the new city."[2]

Yet wearing a name here is not simply an expression of support, such as those who wear the jersey of their favorite football player. Much more is going on here, namely the conflict of two worldviews. Whoever's "name" you wear is a pledge of allegiance to that entity, and throughout Revelation we can see the dichotomy of those who wear the name of the Lamb versus those who wear the name of the Beast (e.g., 14:1 vs. 14:11, 13:17 vs. 22:4).[3] The latter have irrevocably set themselves up in opposition to the Lamb, while the former have declared that, no matter what persecution might happen, they will forever bear witness to the Lamb. Those who declare their support for the Lamb will forever be established, like a pillar, no longer prey to the frightening earthquakes that plague the followers of the Beast.

The church at Philadelphia, then, is the story of the "underdog." In the eyes of those around them, including those claiming to follow the one true God, the church at Philadelphia is worthless, insignificant, and weak. Yet God has promised to make it obvious to their greatest detractors that he loves them. Like the 2016 Cubs, they will forever break the stigma of being "losers"; henceforth they will always bear the name of the ultimate Winner. Churches today, no matter how small, are offered the same opportunity.

---

1   Ibid., 197–198.
2   Witherington, *Revelation*, 107.
3   Osborne, *Revelation*, 198.

QUESTIONS FOR FURTHER DISCUSSION

1. In what ways can a small, less prestigious church be more easily discouraged than a larger church? Yet in what ways can Jesus use such a smaller church in a special way for his kingdom?
2. What does it mean for a particular church to have an "open door" given to them by Jesus? In what way can you, personally, help your church to gain that "open door" and keep it open?

10   LAODICEA—SELF-SUFFICIENT CHURCHES MAKE JESUS WANT TO PUKE

Imagine that you have just spent the bulk of a hot summer day mowing the lawn, trimming the weeds, and painting the house. As the sweat pouring down you does its best to resemble a mini-Niagara Falls, a neighbor comes to you with a glass of water. Gratefully and urgently seizing it, you chug down what you thought was a cold glass of filtered water; instead, what you experience is a disgusting drink of lukewarm water with an extremely bad taste to it. What would your reaction be? Most likely, "to spew it out of your mouth."

As it turns out, this is exactly what Jesus is about to do with the church at Laodicea. Instead of being useful like a refreshing, life-giving "cold" church or a therapeutic, healing "hot" church, their useless self-sufficiency has left a bad taste in Jesus' mouth.

THE BACKGROUND OF LAODICEA

The Lycus valley provided a rich environment for the growth of Anatolian cities. In addition to "offering the easiest route from the Aegean coast to the Anatolian plan",[1] one could travel from Philadelphia to Laodicea (just slightly over 40 miles) "on the same major postal road [that went] from Pergamum through Thyatira, Sardis, and Philadelphia to the Mediterranean."[2]

---

1   Hemer, *Letters to the Seven Churches of Asia*, 179.
2   Osborne, *Revelation*, 201.

Environmentally, the Lycus valley was heavily impacted by volcanic activity, the constant threat of earthquakes, and water supplies that ranged from cool and clear to boiling, many marked by heavy deposits of calcium.[1] Hierapolis, in particular, possessed hot springs that "have formed spectacular petrified cascades almost unique in the world."[2]

The Lycus valley was home to three major cities, each of which had churches established early on: Hierapolis, Colossae, and Laodicea (Colossians 4:13). Each of those cities had, in a sense, her own "claim to fame." Nearby Colossae possessed unbeatable drinking water from her beautiful streams:

> The site of Colossae is carefully described by its modern discoverer, W. J. Hamilton (*Researches*, I.509–13), who notes that three clouded streams join above an ancient bridge and fall together into a chasm lined with travertine deposits of the water. Just below the bridge, however, a clear and pure stream falls in a double cascade into the gorge.[3]

On the other hand, Hierapolis was well-known in antiquity for her hot springs, naturally assumed to provide medicinal benefits. Indeed, sitting in a hot spring bath has traditionally been the ultimate in relaxation and therapy for many cultures (Japan included). For Hierapolis in particular, "The medicinal virtues of its streams are reflected in the local religion …. The city's consequent prosperity as a health center and its obtrusive proximity to Laodicea corroborate this application."[4] Hemer's description of the city (the remains of which he personally visited) would be the envy of many a travel brochure:

> Hot, sparkling waters rise from deep pools on the city-plateau, which they cross in narrow raised channels built of their own deposit of calcium carbonate, and spill over the escarpment edge in white cascades through stepped pools of

---

1 Hemer, *Letters to the Seven Churches of Asia*, 182.
2 Ibid., 182.
3 Ibid., 188.
4 Hemer, *Letters to the Seven Churches of Asia*.

snowy incrustation. The cliff is in full view of Laodicea six miles away.... The waters are said to be 95°F. Springs as hot, or hotter, are found elsewhere in the district, though they do not elsewhere find such visually spectacular expression.[1]

I must stress the importance of the above background information for proper application. As we shall see, both "cold" water and "hot" are desirable characteristics. Common sense alone should dictate that both hot and cold water have their uses, and can thus be positive descriptions of a church in ancient near-eastern culture; lukewarm, however, is desirable for nothing. Much more on this (and the common misinterpretations of this passage) later.

All three cities produced high quality wool; however, Laodicea, with its "soft, raven-black wool," easily outdid the others in both the quality and reputation of her clothing.[2] Indeed, Laodicea could boast of many other superior qualities. She was a center of commerce ("Cicero cashed his bills of exchange there on his arrival … in 51 BC"), and so wealthy that in AD 60 Laodicea apparently refused an offer from the Emperor himself to assist in recovery from an earthquake![3] Finally, Laodicea was also known for a popular eye medicine, "Phrygian powder" and a school for healing linked to "Men Karou" ("the god of healing" for the area).[4]

Laodicea, however, had a major problem. Unlike her sisters, Colossae and Hierapolis, Laodicea was founded without access to a natural water supply. Consequently, she had to pipe in, via aqueduct, water from some source relatively nearby, resulting in lukewarm water.[5] In addition, examination of the ancient aqueducts in the area and the surrounding area in general has attested

---

1 Ibid., 187.
2 Osborne, *Revelation*, 201.
3 Hemer, *Letters to the Seven Churches of Asia*, 191–195.
4 Osborne, *Revelation*, 201.
5 For the details on the "how" and "why" of the lukewarm water, see the informative article by Stanley Porter, "Why the Laodicians Received Lukewarm Water (Revelation 3:15–18)," *TynB* 38 (1987): 143–149. Porter builds off and expands on Hemer's work.

to the overall poor quality of the water, in contrast to that of Colossae.[1]

We see, then, the status of Laodicea as rich, producer of exotic wool, and the developer of famous eye medicines (and thus rather prideful in her attitude), yet lacking in something so incredibly basic that any city would have difficulty functioning without: pure water. Sadly, the church at Laodicea mirrored the attitude of the city—though outwardly self-sufficient, inwardly she was suffering from a foundational spiritual deficiency. Consequently, Jesus confronts his church with "rhetorical irony," demonstrating "through ironical words and images" that a surface glimpse of the church does not do justice to her inward reality.[2]

JESUS' MESSAGE TO LAODICEA

In Jesus' opening self-designation in 3:14, we see the familiar phrase "the faithful witness," echoing the language of 1:5 and continuing the major theme of Jesus as the ultimate witness/testimony. Interestingly, however, we also see Jesus as "The Amen" and "the ruler of God's creation" (here I prefer "ruler," with the NIV, rather than "beginning," with the KJV; see the note for further discussion).[3] Quite possibly, as G. K. Beale argues, the background for these two unique expressions is a combination of Isaiah 65:15–16 and 43:10–12. Jesus, then, in Revelation may be portrayed as the "faithful witness" to God's "new creation" in those Isaiah passages (see esp. Isaiah 65:17–18), ultimately linked to Jesus' own resur-

---

1 Hemer, *Letters to the Seven Churches of Asia*, 189–190.
2 Witherington, *Revelation*, 108.
3 The Greek word *archē* can mean either "beginning" (Matthew 19:4) or "ruler" (Luke 12:11). When speaking of *people*, however, it is natural to take the noun in reference to one having authority, i.e., a "ruler" (e.g., 1 Corinthians 15:24, Colossians 1:16, etc.) Admittedly, however, the expression "I am the Alpha and the Omega, the Beginning [*archē*] and the End," which occurs three times in the Greek of the *Textus Receptus* of Revelation, would be an exception (though context clearly disambiguates, in those cases). Also, for Revelation 3:14, "the preeminent one" would be a legitimate possibility in light of how the word is used in Acts 26:4.

rection (see Revelation 1:5, as well as parallels in Colossians 1:15 and 18b).[1] Yet if we take the Greek *archē* to mean "ruler" instead of "beginning," then we also see Jesus' kingly authority, as the ultimate witness to God, to rule over the creation that he redeems.

Appropriately, the promise to the overcomers given in 3:21 involves ruling alongside of Jesus Christ. Since Jesus is the High King over all creation, he consequently has the right to appoint men and women to rule over creation as Adam and Eve were meant to.[2] This theme is continued in Revelation 5:8–10, where the Lamb designates the 24 elders to be "kings and priests" in order to rule on earth.

With this reminder of his regal authority over all creation, that he alone has the right to pass judgment, Jesus Christ now confronts the believers in Laodicea. The controlling metaphor here in Jesus' judgment is "water" (what else would you "spew out of your mouth"?), and clearly Jesus views both "cold" and "hot" as desirable alternatives to "lukewarm." The reason, as we have seen, is that both "cold" water and "hot" water have a valuable function in this Mediterranean environment. The reason is not, as is often preached, because Jesus prefers somebody totally hostile to the Gospel over somebody who has accepted the Gospel but is not wholeheartedly following Jesus. How would that even make sense?

The problem is that we have allowed English idioms of "cold" and "hot" to color our perception of Jesus' message. For modern American society, an athlete who is "hot" is "on fire" for their team (with a hitting streak, consecutive touchdown passes, or whatever) while an athlete who is "cold" is in a slump. Elsewhere in English, "hot" is positive (e.g., a colloquialism in describing somebody attractive) while "cold" is negative (somebody gave me "the cold shoulder"). Yet this is *not* what Jesus is talking about. His audience is 1st century Anatolian, not 21st century American. To truly un-

---

1   Beale, *Book of Revelation*, 297–298.
2   Once again, for a helpful discussion of the original "commission" of Adam as a steward-ruler of God's garden, see Beale, *New Testament Biblical Theology*, 30–39.

derstand Jesus' message, we must not neglect the background, i.e., the time and place that his message is directed to. Only then can we apply it to ourselves.

Furthermore, a little common sense is all one needs: is cold water good or bad? Obviously good! The only other place this particular word for "cold" (Greek *psuchros*) is used in the New Testament is Matthew 10:42, where whoever gives a cup of cold water to a disciple is blessed.[1]

Jesus, then, is saying that unlike cold water and hot water, the Laodicean church is useless to him. Osborne summarizes it best:

> The Laodiceans should have been known for their spiritual healing (like Hierapolis) or their refreshing, life-giving ministry (like Colossae). Instead, as Jesus' next statement reads, they were 'lukewarm.' They were devoid of works and useless to the Lord.... The exalted Christ is challenging them with a powerful rhetorical question, 'Don't you realize that you make me sick?'[2]

The theme of spiritual "water," of course, resounds all throughout Revelation. In 7:17, those redeemed during the great tribulation are promised the Lamb himself as a shepherd who leads them to "living fountains of water" (deliberately echoing Psalm 23). In contrast, in 8:10, the "fountains of water" (same two words as in 7:17) left on earth will be polluted by the "great star from heaven," Wormwood. In 14:7, the nations of the earth are called to worship the very one who made those "fountains of water" (again, same words). The ending of Revelation, however, twice invites all humanity to freely partake of those living streams of water (21:6, 22:17; cf. 22:1–3). The true Living Water that Jesus Christ offers

---

1 The English word "cold" occurs elsewhere in both the KJV and NIV, but in those cases it is a different Greek word; this particular word in both Matt 10:42 and Revelation 3:15–16 seems to be tied more closely to drinking water, e.g., as seen in its use in LXX Proverbs 25:25 (a verse describing the pleasure of cold water).
2 Osborne, *Revelation*, 206.

causes one to become a member of the Kingdom of God, infinitely surpassing the lukewarm water that the world offers.

So why, then, did Jesus declare the Laodicean church to be as worthless as lukewarm water? The answer is clearly given in verse 17. They assumed they had all they needed, and had inadvertently shut out Jesus Christ (which is why he is left knocking at the door in v. 20). Most likely, as Alan Johnson points out, "The Laodiceans may have interpreted their material wealth as a blessing from God and thus have been self-deceived as to their true spiritual state."[1] Yet such a church, which has allowed material "blessing" to seduce it into self-sufficiency, has inadvertently mimicked the nations of Psalm 2, seeking to throw off the "chains" of servitude to the King of Kings, imagining a "vain thing," namely that they do not need the Anointed One. Self-sufficiency, then, is the most pagan of attitudes; to borrow language from Dickens' classic *A Christmas Carol*, the church at Laodicea has replaced their true love with "an idol . . . a golden one."[2] In this way the church has become almost as pagan as those around her. Yet just as the Lord "laughs to scorn" the ungodly nations in Psalm 2:4–5, so also Jesus will "vomit out" the Laodicean church. The question is, how many modern "rich" churches will Jesus also spew out along with Laodicea?

Jesus' call to repentance in verse 18 ("buy real gold, buy superior clothing, use spiritual eye medicine") all plays off of the background of the city as rich, maker of fantastic clothing, and developer of excellent eye medicine. Assuming that their material wealth makes them important, the Laodicean church, like the ruler in the story of "The Emperor's New Clothes," failed to see that in reality they were spiritually as naked as a jaybird. Osborne brilliantly puts it this way, as a lesson to all of us: "It is possible to

---

[1] Alan Johnson, "Revelation," in vol. 12 of *The Expositor's Bible Commentary* (Grand Rapids, MI: Zondervan, 1981), 458.
[2] Language borrowed from Charles Dickens, *A Christmas Carol* (London: Chapman & Hall, 1843), n.p. Online: https://www.gutenberg.org/files/46/46-h/46-h.htm.

wear Armani suits and Dior dresses but to be 'naked' in the eyes of God."[1]

Furthermore, in light of the fact that Laodicea was so rich they actually refused their emperor's aid for help, we can see that the Laodicean church is "exposed as partaking of the standards of the society in which it lived. It was spiritually self-sufficient and saw no need of Christ's aid."[2] Such self-sufficiency is the height of arrogance. Osborne aptly points us to "the preponderance of first-person singulars in their claims: 'I am ... I have ... I have.' Their boastful pride and self-sufficiency rendered them 'blind' to the truth."[3]

In a sense, the entirety of Revelation is about those nations in Psalm 2 who declare their self-sufficiency, their desire to be independent from the Messiah. Indeed, the ultimate expression of self-sufficiency is to turn from the Son of Man to the Beast, the one who will manifest the ultimate of democratic ideals, "choosing one's own path," doing whatever it takes to once-for-all declare independence from the one true God.[4] In 14:7–9, we have the ultimate choice facing humanity: glorify and reverence God, or worship the Beast (by taking his mark). Humans are given the very real option of once-for-all turning their back on the Son of Man, the "ruler of God's creation," yet in doing so they stand condemned forever. They get their wish: they no longer have to answer to God. In consequence, however, they place themselves outside of the Light and into darkness forever.

We see, then, that when a church claims "I am rich and don't need anything," this is not a "casual" sin that receives a simple slap on the hand. With such a declaration, the church has aligned itself

---

1 Osborne, *Revelation*, 209.
2 Hemer, *Letters to the Seven Churches of Revelation*, 195.
3 Osborne, *Revelation*, 207.
4 For a fascinating discussion (over a hundred years ago) on how the Beast, in a sense, is "the full evolution of the democratic idea," see Samuel J. Andrews, *Christianity and Anti-Christianity in Their Final Conflict* (Chicago: Bible Institute Colportage,1890), xvii. I am grateful to my friend Joe Henson for pointing me to this source.

with the pagan nations of the world in opposition to Jesus Christ. For one to say to Jesus "We have no need of you" is essentially to say, "We don't know you."

Fortunately, Jesus Christ offers hope. Though he threatens to spew this church out of his mouth, he is still knocking at the door to be let in. As Ernst Lohmeyer indicates, this is not the harsh knocking of master returning to punish his lazy servants, but rather that of a friend from a foreign country, knocking and expecting hospitality.[1]

The emphasis in 3:20 on "anyone" seems to indicate that Jesus wishes for a relationship with each person, individually (though certainly with broader application to the church; the church does not change unless the individuals change).[2] Whether or not this is an "evangelistic" verse *per se* depends on how one views the church at Laodicea, either as believers in need of a sanctifying work ("revival"), or unbelievers, "fakers," in need of repentance.[3] Regardless, we are struck with the irony that, just like Laodicea thought she could boast of her riches while not possessing even a basic water supply, so also the Laodicean church thought she could boast of spiritual maturity while having locked out the Living Water, who yet continues to knock for admittance.

---

1 Ernst Lohmeyer, *Die Offenbarung des Johannes* (Tübingen: Mohr-Siebeck, 1926), 37. Lohmeyer sees this verse as simultaneously "present" and "eschatological." Also, Walvoord focuses on the personal side of this verse and downplays the eschatological, noting correctly that "It is hardly true that at His Second Coming Christ will knock at the door and invite men to let Him in. The picture here seems more applicable to the present, when Christ remains on the outside unless He is welcomed" (*Revelation of Jesus Christ*, 98).
2 Hemer, *Letters to the Seven Churches of Revelation*, 207.
3 Many would see Laodicea as an "apostate church" (I am borrowing this terminology from my father, John Himes) where the majority, if not most, of the individuals are not born again (e.g., Walvoord, *Revelation of Jesus Christ*, 99; Johnson, "Revelation," 459). For one of the more helpful discussions on Revelation 3:20, see Tim Wiarda, "Revelation 3:20: Imagery and Literary Context," *JETS* 38.2 (June 1995): 203–212.

In this letter we close with Jesus, the ruler, offering the opportunity to rule alongside of him. Each of the letters to Revelation in essence ends with an invitation ("he who has an ear, let him hear …"). Jesus is still knocking at the hearts of humanity, and sends out his messengers with a wedding banquet invitation to drink of the Living Water which, apparently, Laodicea lacked (Revelation 22:17).

One more closing point: in the final invitation of Revelation 22:17, Jesus indicates that the Spirit and the Bride bear an invitation to humanity. However, he goes further than that—"the one hearing" (i.e., the one listening to Revelation being read) is also the bearer of good news! John thus echoes the Great Commission, namely that those who *hear* the Good News are also obligated to *declare* the Good News. Followers of Jesus Christ are united with him in the mission of reclaiming humanity, of offering healing to the nations. "Even so come, Lord Jesus!"

EXCURSUS: THE MOST MISINTERPRETED VERSE IN REVELATION 1–3

While I cannot speak for other Christian groups, in my own independent Baptist circles the "cold, hot, and lukewarm" of Revelation 3:15–16 is usually preached as a reference to being "sold out for God" (or not), i.e., spiritual zealousness. The "hot" are those who are "on fire" for God while the "cold" are, apparently, unbelievers. Such an understanding lacks both common sense (is cold water bad?) and an ignorance of the background of Laodicea, in addition to resulting in the theological absurdity that an unbeliever is more favorable in the eyes of God than a less-than-stellar believer (what, then, did Jesus' atoning work accomplish?) As Johnson aptly states, "It is inconceivable that Christ would wish that people were spiritually cold, or unsaved and hostile."[1]

I repeat, then: preaching that Jesus' water metaphor refers to how much one is "sold out to God" completely ignores what Jesus is actually saying. Jesus makes it clear that this church's uselessness

---

1   Johnson, "Revelation," 457.

Where Is Your Allegiance?

as lukewarm water stems from their self-sufficiency. This may or may not go hand-in-hand, in practice, with "not being sold out for God," though in my experience there have been plenty of people who considered themselves "sold out for God" yet were arrogant and self-sufficient (we may also mention the Apostle Paul, pre-conversion, who certainly did not lack for zealousness!). Ultimately, however, the concept of whether or not one is "zealous" for God is irrelevant to the text. The point is self-sufficiency, and the pastor who preaches this text as a polemic against lack of zealousness is missing the point.

Fortunately, among my own ecclesiastical circles I have seen evidence of a change. I recently heard an excellent sermon by an evangelist out of Kansas City who fully acknowledged that he used to interpret this passage incorrectly before realizing the absurdity of "cold" as a reference to the unbeliever. I have seen indications that others, with various degrees of education, are starting to see the point of the passage and not merely parroting what they've heard preached.

Indeed, understanding the "cold," "hot," and "lukewarm" reference does not require a graduate degree in Bible. Some years ago a very good friend of mine, a layman in his church with a bachelor's in business, was asked to do a Bible study on Revelation and through his own research came to the conclusion that the "temperature as zealous fervor" view was wrong (putting him a step ahead, in my opinion, of many preachers). In other words, one does not need a Bible degree to effectively study the Bible!

The problem, in my opinion, is that many preachers of the Word have become too comfortable with "Christian clichés," passed down from one homiletical generation to the next, clichés that may not actually reflect what the Bible is saying. Generations of preachers in my own Baptist circles have consistently preached "hot is good, cold is bad, and lukewarm means 'not on fire for God'" from Revelation 3:15–16 simply because that is what they heard from their favorite preacher, when simple common sense ("cold water is good!") and knowledge of the city's background (knowledge that is not too difficult to acquire) shows otherwise. Sometimes we love our clichés too much to allow ourselves to approach Scripture from a fresh perspective.

QUESTIONS FOR FURTHER DISCUSSION

1. In what ways are North American churches, especially, prone to the sin of self-sufficiency? What are some ways that this can be guarded against?
2. Positively, in what ways can a church work on being either like cold water (refreshing, life-giving) or like hot water (relaxing, therapeutic)?

11 How Should We Respond?

The study of John's Apocalypse provides an incredibly rewarding (and often bizarre) experience for devoted students of God's word. At the highest academic levels, much work still remains to be done on the theology, language, intertextuality, and even the genre of Revelation.

Yet Revelation was not written so that scholars could publish even more academic monographs and dozens more technical articles per year. All those have their place, but they do not make us "spiritual." Ultimately, Revelation "was meant to be read in the context of Christian faith, and it was meant to be obeyed, not merely studied."[1] In other words, we have not truly begun to understand Revelation until we have begun to obey Jesus' words in Revelation. One may have a Ph.D. in New Testament and have completely read through Revelation in Greek, with access to the best commentaries, yet if the words of Jesus and John make no impact on such a person's life, then that knowledge is worthless. Worse still, he or she will be held accountable to a greater degree than one who has never read Revelation! Conversely, somebody with minimal education may read Revelation, be genuinely puzzled by all the "beasts" and "asteroids" and so forth, yet do his or her best to obey what is understandable; such a person will invariably come away with a deeper sense of loyalty to the High King, Jesus the Messiah. Such a person will receive a superior seat at the Lamb's banquet than those of us with fancy degrees, if we neglect to live out what we discover.

---

1 Witherington, *Revelation*, 111.

First and foremost, then, the message of the first three chapters of Revelation is about our relationship with Jesus Christ. We are who we are because of who he is and what he has done. Since he was resurrected, we also will be resurrected. Since he overcomes, we will also overcome (if we are truly born of God). Since he reigns, we also may reign. Since he is the ultimate witness to God, we also can be (and must be) witnesses to the Lamb. Since he confronts us as the divine and fearsome Son of Man, we must bow to him in humble submission, hearing and obeying what he has to say.

We see throughout Revelation a major conflict between the Lamb and his followers and the Beast and his followers. While the Beast is allowed to "overcome" believers at first (to all outward appearances), in reality it is believers themselves who "overcome" the Beast with their testimony. When the Lamb reappears, the Beast is utterly destroyed, and the Lamb will establish his kingdom once for all on the earth, redeeming the nations in the process and silencing the rebellion of Psalm 2. The curse will be reversed, the Garden of Eden will be restored, and the redeemed nations will orbit around the ultimate capital city, the New Jerusalem. The superiority of the Lamb, the Son of Man, is trumpeted all throughout Revelation, so that all humanity knows that Jesus, the Jewish Messiah, is not merely one rival god among many, slowly pulling himself to the top, but rather the (past, present, future) Sovereign Lord over all creation, who laughs scornfully at the mere idea of rivals.

The Lamb's message to the churches is written in the context of the Greco-Roman empire and its power in Asia Minor. The nations of the earth have submitted (quite often willingly) to the *pax Romana*, and Rome herself has become to them a goddess worthy of worship (a worship that was transferred then to the emperors). The claims of both Rome and Caesar to be the Savior of the World, Lord and god, etc., stand in irreconcilable opposition to the Son of Man. Rome and Caesar, in turn, represent a future figure yet to come who will essentially offer an upgraded Roman Empire in opposition to the Kingdom of Heaven. Then, as now and in the past, humanity will be forced to make a choice: either throw off the "yoke," the "servitude" that the Son of Man demands and enjoy the "freedom" that the Beast offers (freedom that leads to destruction), or fix their eyes on the crucified and resurrected Lamb, the atoning Savior, pledging allegiance to him in opposition to all competing loyalties. Only by becoming a servant of the Lamb does one experience true freedom, freedom to accomplish what humanity was meant to accomplish, stewards of God's creation and heralds of his glory.

Approaching the seven churches as their sovereign Lord, the Lamb critiques them on their performance. Some receive praise, some receive criticism, and some receive both. On the positive side, Jesus offers strong encouragement to churches who are suffering. As we have seen, Antipas the martyr is our role model here (next to Jesus himself), and churches that are suffering for their allegiance to Jesus Christ become the example for all other churches to emulate. In the midst of the hatred, mockery, and physical abuse, the people who hold fast to their witness for Jesus Christ will be labeled "the Overcomers," and will rule with the Son over the earth at his coming. This, indeed, is the biggest cause for praise in Revelation 2–3: perseverance under pressure. I believe we Americans will be amazed to see how many Chinese, Indians, Africans, and Middle Easterners enter the Banquet ahead of us. While we have had our opportunity to enjoy primacy, wealth, and social acceptance, at the Lamb's banquet "the last will be first."

Furthermore, churches are encouraged to strongly oppose both theological and practical compromise. Ephesus is strongly commended for being "intolerant," as the world might define it. In other words, Ephesus refused to acknowledge certain alternative theological beliefs as equally valid next to the core Faith handed down from the apostles and Jesus himself. There must be a line drawn in the sand that cannot be crossed: believers may genuinely and cordially disagree about many things, but not the core concepts of the Gospel. In addition, allegiance to the crucified and resurrected Messiah is not optional for those claiming to be part of the church.

Yet while key doctrines must not be denied, neither can Christian practice (e.g., reverence of Jesus Christ) be wedded to pagan practices (reverence of the emperor or the pagan gods). One cannot reverence both Jesus and the emperor. While the emperor does not make exclusive claims (to be the *only* "savior," for example), the former does. Jesus declares, "I alone am the Savior of the Cosmos, and there can be only one!" To offer sacrifices to, or even to participate in a meal dedicated to reverencing any entity other than the Triune God, is to deny Jesus' exclusive claim to our allegiance. The same can be said regarding any boasting that we are "100% for" any mere human. The Lamb refuses to take second place.

Sadly, one of the major failures plaguing the seven churches consists of practical compromise. In order to avoid standing out like a sore thumb, some professing believers were advocating participating in pagan reverence and pagan immorality. This is tantamount to a denial of the Lamb's sovereign rule above all others. Those who make such compromises will find themselves at war with the Lamb.

Although Thyatira is commended for her love, Ephesus on the other hand is rebuked for losing it. Even in the midst of theological (and practical) orthodoxy, it is possible for a church to completely derail off the tracks by forgetting to love Jesus and each other. Furthermore, talk is cheap; love is evidenced by "works," and unless Ephesus demonstrates those "works" of love, she faces dire consequences.

Lack of diligence, i.e., overall carelessness, can also cause a church to go downhill. We are left wondering what, exactly, was Sardis' problem, yet the solution to avoiding it most likely consists of prayer that we will not let ourselves slack off in any of the Christian virtues we must partake in (indeed, how can God *not* answer such a prayer if prayed in sincerity?), as well as consistent self-examination.

Finally, self-sufficiency, and the arrogance which accompany it, make a church utterly despicable in the eyes of Jesus. When believers become so caught up in who they are and what they are doing, as well as focusing on material wealth as a sure sign of God's pleasure, with the result that they forget they need Jesus, such a church makes Jesus sick to the stomach. The solution is humility and hearkening to the voice of the One knocking outside the door (both the door to the church and the door to one's own heart).

Naturally, different churches in different parts of the world may need to pay more attention to some of the letters than to others. A persecuted church in modern China, for example, may need to make sure they are not tolerating compromise in the midst of their persecution, while a church in North America may need to make sure they are not another Laodicea. However, each letter has something for everyone. Furthermore, change starts in the heart of individuals. We must not shake our finger in rebuke at others while failing to examine our own hearts. Only once we have humbled ourselves, and consequently evidence proactive change in our own lives and in our relationship to our brothers and sisters—only then can we make a positive difference in our local church.

One final point: Jesus, when confronting the churches, demands repentance and action. Failure to do so means that Jesus himself will take action. In other words, if we, as a church, don't take care of our problems, Jesus will! This sobering thought should drive us to consistently examine our own hearts so that we can determine who, or what, truly has our allegiance.

Personal Exercises

Exercise #1:

Examine your own life. Imagine if Christians in your city all resembled you, personally. What would a letter from the Messiah to the church in your city look like? (Here's a hint: if such a letter would be exclusively positive, then we probably haven't examined our own hearts accurately enough. On the other hand, we should not be too hard on ourselves, either. We're all still growing in grace, and Jesus still loves us!).

Exercise #2:

Having examined your own life and humbled yourself, now write a letter to the churches in your city based on what you know about local Christians in general. Like Jesus, draw on the background elements of your city for metaphors and analogies. Include both positive and negative elements (and be sure to offer hope).

Exercise #3:

Now focus on the Christians in your country as a whole. What are the positive elements? Negative? For example, a country that is well-known for sending out missionaries to other countries should be commended for that, yet may also need to be rebuked if its ability to do so reflects a prosperity which, in turn, has led to arrogance or complacency. Once again, utilize the history and background of your country for analogies and metaphors.

APPENDIX A

Resources for Further Study

Dear reader, if this book has stoked up a desire to study the rest of Revelation, then all my labor has been worth it (conversely, if this book has caused you to run away, despairing of ever understanding Revelation, then I have miserably failed!). Revelation, probably more than any other book, has caused theological controversy among godly believers, and thus offers a greater challenge for even the most diligent students of God's Word.

In the following paragraphs I offer you a brief overview of some of the more helpful scholarly material. I do not cover "devotional" material or casual commentaries. Many of those are spiritually profitable to some degree, and (granting my bias) I must here offer my own great-grandfather's book as a positive example, without endorsing all of it (John R. Rice, *Behold He Cometh: A Verse-By-Verse Commentary on the Book of Revelation* [Murfreesboro, TN: Sword of the Lord, 1977]). Generally, however, devotional books don't *teach*; rather, they encourage or challenge. Granted, we all need that; my point, however, is that devotional books will generally not help you come to a deeper understanding of the message (and difficulties) of Revelation.

With that in mind, I offer this brief guide for serious study.

First of all, if you can only afford one commentary, you should purchase Grant R. Osborne, *Revelation*, in the Baker Exegetical Commentary series (Grand Rapids, MI: Baker Academic, 2002). I say this despite the fact that Osborne does not reflect my own theological position on many issues; in other words, this is an unbiased recommendation—Osborne is the best commentary for serious study regardless of whether or not I agree with him! Although somewhat technical, this book is not actually as difficult to read as you would expect (Osborne is an excellent writer and researcher; in addition, he quite often makes spiritual application).

So I recommend Osborne, then, for all who wish for serious study, no matter what their theological persuasion. My other recommended commentaries, however, will be somewhat subject to my reader's own views on eschatology. Before we get to that point, I would also recommend two non-commentaries. For background study, Colin J. Hemer, *The Letters to the Seven Churches of Asia in Their Local Setting* (Grand Rapids, MI: Eerdmans, 1986) is absolutely essential (and I cite him frequently in this book). For a theological overview, Richard Bauckham, *The Theology of the Book of Revelation*, New Testament Theology series (Cambridge: Cambridge University Press, 1993), is the classic work, still unparalleled (and one of the more easily-readable books on this list).

Now back to commentaries. If you are a Dispensationalist, the most scholarly commentary would be the two volume set by Robert L. Thomas, *Revelation 1–7: An Exegetical Commentary* and *Revelation 8–22: An Exegetical Commentary*, in the Wycliffe Exegetical Commentary series (Chicago, IL: Moody, 1992 and 1995). If you wish for something a bit more reader-friendly and less intimidating, then John F. Walvoord, *The Revelation of Jesus Christ* (Chicago, IL: Moody, 1966) is considered the "classic" dispensationalist commentary, significantly less technical than many of the others on the list (it is also probably the best-selling book on this list).

For those of a Reformed persuasion, since I have considerable respect for Vern S. Poythress, I would recommend *The Returning King: A Guide to the Book of Revelation* (Phillipsburg, NJ: P&R, 2000). In addition, G. K. Beale's *Revelation: A Shorter Commentary*, written with David Campbell (Grand Rapids, MI: Eerdmans, 2015), is an excellent resource from the Reformed perspective.

Beale's longer commentary, *The Book of Revelation*, in the New International Greek Testament Commentary series (Grand Rapids, MI: Eerdmans, 2013) should be tackled only by those proficient in the biblical languages. It remains a valuable technical resource, though I much prefer Osborne as my "go-to" book for serious study.

Other beneficial commentaries, regardless of eschatological orientation, would include the following: Robert H. Mounce, *The Book of Revelation*, NICNT (Grand Rapids, MI: Eerdmans, 1997); Craig S. Keener, *Revelation*, NIVAppC (Grand Rapids, MI: Zondervan, 2000); Paige Patterson, *Revelation: An Exegetical and Theological Exposition of Holy Scripture*, NAC (Nashville, TN: B&H, 2012); and Ben Witherington III, *Revelation*, NCBC (Cambridge: Cambridge University Press, 2003).

In general, for the Christian without seminary training who wishes to expand his or her library with commentaries that combine scholarship, readability, and spiritual application, I would especially recommend the NIV Application Commentary series (published by Zondervan). This series makes a concerted effort to actually speak to the challenges of living the Christian life, yet does so on the basis of solid Christian scholarship. While I have not read every book in the series, I would especially recommend both George Guthrie on Hebrews and Scot McKnight on 1 Peter.

Finally, I will give a fairly positive (though mixed) recommendation to one particular book (also noting that it is well-written, easily readable, and has plenty of pictures!): J. Nelson Kraybill, *Apocalypse and Allegiance: Worship, Politics, and Devotion in the Book of Revelation* (Grand Rapids, MI: Brazos, 2010). I suspect my eschatology is significantly different from that of Kraybill, and I only cite his work once in this book; nevertheless, there is much here on the nature of "allegiance" and the supremacy of Jesus Christ that resonates strongly with what I wrote (though I came to my conclusions separately). Furthermore, Kraybill's book is very deep on background material (and did I mention it has plenty of pictures?).

This list, of course, is barely the tip of the iceberg, and I have neglected many "oldies-but-goodies." Nevertheless, I hope that I have given you a solid starting point for serious study on the book, with the understanding that the entire space-time continuum of the universe does not contain enough time or space to exhaust our study of the eternal Lamb and his revelation. To Him and the eternal Father be glory for ever and ever, through the eternal Spirit, Amen!

Bibliography

Andrews, Samuel J. *Christianity and Anti-Christianity in Their Final Conflict*. Chicago: Bible Institute Colportage, 1890.

Baker, Richard Terrill. *Darkness of the Sun: The Story of Christianity in the Japanese Empire*. New York: Abingdon-Cokesbury, 1947.

Bandy, Alan S. "Patterns of Prophetic Lawsuits in the Oracles to the Seven Churches." *Neotestamentica* 45.2 (2011): 178–205.

Barth, Markus, and Verne H. Fletcher. *Acquittal by Resurrection*. New York: Holdt, Rinehart, and Winston, 1964.

Bauckham, Richard. *The Theology of the Book of Revelation*. New Testament Theology. Cambridge: Cambridge University Press, 1993.

Beale, G. K. *A New Testament Biblical Theology: The Unfolding of the Old Testament in the New*. Grand Rapids, MI: Baker Academic, 2011.

———. *The Book of Revelation*. New International Greek Testament Commentary. Grand Rapids, MI: Eerdmans, 1999.

———. *We Become What We Worship: A Biblical Theology of Idolatry*. Downers Grove, IL: InterVarsity, 2008.

Bellamy, Francis. "Companion Address to the Pledge of Allegiance." Pages 662–663 of *Holy-Days and Holidays: A Treasury of Historical Material in Full and Brief, Suggestive Thoughts, and Poetry, Relating to Holy Days and Holidays*. New York: Funk and Wagnalls, 1902. Text also available online at http://undergod.procon.org/view.additional-resource.php?resourceID=78, cited 30 July 2015.

Bettler, John F. "Guidelines from II Timothy for Counseling People with Fear." *Westminster Theological Journal* 26.2 (1974): 198–208.

Black, David Alan. *Christian Archy*. Critical Christian Issues. Gonzalez, FL: Energion, 2009.

Blomberg, Craig L. "The New Testament Definition of Heresy (Or When Do Jesus and the Apostles Really Get Mad?)," *Journal of the Evangelical Theological Society* 45.1 (March 2002): 59–72.

Bosler, Bobby. "The Comfort Continuum." Sermon preached on 1 Nov 2016 at Baptist College of Ministry (Menomonee Falls, WI).

Burge, Gary M., Lynn H. Cohick, and Gene L. Green. *The New Testament in Antiquity: A Survey of the New Testament within Its Cultural Contexts*. Grand Rapids, MI: Zondervan, 2009.

Collins, Brian. "The Land Promise in Scripture." Paper presented at the Bible Faculty Summit. Watertown, WI. 27 July 2016.

Davids, Peter H. *Living in the Light of the Coming King: A Theology of James, Peter, and Jude*. Biblical Theology of the New Testament. Grand Rapids, MI: Zondervan 2014.

deSilva, David A. "Honor Discourse and the Rhetorical Strategy of the Apocalypse of John." *Journal for the Study of the New Testament* 71 (1998): 79–110.

———. *Seeing Things John's Way: The Rhetoric of the Book of Revelation*. Louisville, KY: Westminster John Knox, 2009.

Dickens, Charles. *A Christmas Carol*. London: Chapman & Hall, 1843.

Estes, Daniel. "Poetic Artistry in the Expression of Fear in Psalm 49." *Bibliotheca Sacra* 161 (Jan 2004): 55–71.

"Extracts from a Diploma of Club Membership" (P. Brit. Mus. 1178). Ed. and trans. by George Milligan. Cambridge: Cambridge University Press, 1912. Reprinted by Forgotten Books, 2015.

Feldmeier, Reinhard. "Die Außenseiter als savant-garde Gesellschaftliche Ausgrenzung als Missionarische Chance nach dem 1. Petrusbrief." Pages 161–178 in *Persuasion and Dissuasion in Early Christianity, Ancient Judaism, and Hellenism*. Eds. Pieter W. van der Horst, M. J. J. Menken, J. F. M. Smit, and Geert Van Oyen. Contributions to Bibilcal Exegesis and Theology 33. Leuven: Peeters, 2003.

Ferguson, Everett. "Angels of the Churches in Revelation 1–3: *Status Quaestionis* and Another Proposal." *Bulletin for Biblical Research* 21.3 (2011): 371–386.

Fishwick, Duncan. *The Imperial Cult in the Latin West*. Vol. 1 of *Studies in the Ruler Cult of the Western Provinces of the Roman Empire*. Leiden: E. J. Brill, 1993.

Greek New Testament: Textus Receptus (1550). Edited by Robert Estienne. Compiled by Maurice Robinson. Accessed via *Accordance* 11.1.6. OakTree Software, 2016.

Hattaway, Paul. *China's Book of Martyrs: AD 845-Present*. Vol. 1 of *The Church in China*. Carlisle, CA: Piquant, 2007.

Hemer, Colin J. *The Letters to the Seven Churches of Asia in Their Local Setting*. Biblical Resource Series. Grand Rapids, MI: Eerdmans, 1989.

Hoehner, Harold W. *Ephesians: An Exegetical Commentary*. Grand Rapids, MI: Baker Academic, 2002.

Humphrey, Edith M. *And I Turned to See the Voice: The Rhetoric of Vision in the New Testament*. Studies in Theological Interpretation. Grand Rapids, MI: Baker Academic, 2007.

Hurtado, Larry W. *Destroyer of the Gods: Early Christian Distinctiveness in the Roman World*. Waco, TX: Baylor University Press, 2016.

———. "The Distinctiveness of Early Christianity." *Catalyst*. No pages. Cited 26 November 2016. Online: http://www.catalystresources.org/the-distinctiveness-of-early-christianity/.

Johnson, Alan. "Revelation." Pages 397–603 in vol. 12 of *The Expositor's Bible Commentary*. Grand Rapids, MI: Zondervan, 1981.

Johnson, Richard Warren. "Confronting the Beast: The Imperial Cult and the Book of Revelation." Pages 130–144 in *Essays on Revelation: Appropriating Yesterday's Apocalypse in Today's World*. Ed. Gerald L. Stevens. Eugene, OR: Pickwick, 2010.

Josephus, *Jewish Antiquities*. Greek text based on the 1890 Niese edition. English text from *The Works of Josephus: Complete and Unabridged*. Ed. and trans. by William Whiston. New Updated Edition. Peabody, MA: Hendrickson, Accessed via *Accordance* 11.1.6. OakTree Software, 2016.

Komoszewski, J. Ed., M. James Sawyer, and Daniel B. Wallace. *Reinventing Jesus: How Contemporary Skeptics Miss the Real Jesus and Mislead Popular Culture*. Grand Rapids, MI: Kregel, 2006.

Kraybill, J. Nelson. *Apocalypse and Allegiance: Worship, Politics, and Devotion in the Book of Revelation*. Grand Rapids, MI: Brazos, 2010.

Lohmeyer, Ernst. *Die Offenbarung des Johannes*. Tübingen: Mohr-Siebeck, 1926.

McNicol, Allan J. *The Conversion of the Nations in Revelation*. Library of New Testament Studies 438. London: T&T Clark, 2011.

Miller, Stephen R. *Daniel: An Exegetical and Theological Exposition of Holy Scripture*. New American Commentary. Nashville, TN: B&H, 1994.

Mitchell, Stephen. *The Celts and the Impact of Roman Rule*. Vol. 1 of *Anatolia: Land, Men, and Gods in Asia Minor*. Oxford: Clarendon, 1993.

Novum Testamentum Graecae. Edited by Barbara Aland and Kurt Aland. 27th ed. Stuttgart, Germany: Deutsche Bibelgesellschaft, 1993. Accessed via *Accordance* 11.1.6. OakTree Software, 2016.

Osborne, Grant R. *Revelation*. Baker Exegetical Commentary on the New Testament. Grand Rapids, MI: Baker Academic, 2002.

Pliny the Younger. *Letters*. Translated by William Whiston. Peabody, MA: Hendrickson, 1987. Online: http://www.pbs.org/wgbh/pages/frontline/shows/religion/maps/primary/pliny.html.

Polybius. *Histories*. Translated by W. R. Paton. Loeb Classical Library, vol. 3. Cambridge, MA: Harvard University Press, 1923. Online: http://penelope.uchicago.edu/Thayer/E/Roman/Texts/Polybius/7*.html.

Porter, Stanley. "Why the Laodiceans Received Lukewarm Water (Revelation 3:15–18)." *Tyndale Bulletin* 38 (1987): 143–149.

Price, S. R. F. *Rituals and Power: The Roman Imperial Cult in Asia Minor*. Cambridge: Cambridge University Press, 1984.

Schröger, Friedrich. *Gemeinde im 1. Petrusbrief: Untersuchungen zum Selbstverständnis einer christlichen Gemeinde an der Wende vom 1. zum 2. Jahrhundert*. Katholische Theologie. Passau: Passavia Universtätslage, 1981.

Slater, Thomas B. *Christ and Community: A Socio-Historical Study of the Christology of Revelation*. Journal for the Study of the New Testament Supplement Series 178. Sheffield, England: Sheffield Academic, 1999.

Steveson, Peter A. *A Commentary on Isaiah*. Greenville, SC: BJU Press, 2003.

Suetonius. *The Life of Claudius*. Translated by J. C. Rolfe. Loeb Classical Library. Cambridge, MA: Harvard University Press, 1914. Online: http://penelope.uchicago.edu/Thayer/E/Roman/Texts/Suetonius/12Caesars/Claudius*.html.

The Joshua Project. No pages. Cited 24 November 2016. Online: https://joshuaproject.net/global_list/countries

The New Testament in the Original Greek (Byzantine Textform 2005). Edited by Maurice A. Robinson and William G. Pierpont. Southborough, MA: Chilton, 2005.

Thielman, Frank S. *A New Testament Biblical Theology: A Canonical and Synthetic Approach.* Grand Rapids, MI: Zondervan, 2005.

———. "The Atonement." Pages 102–127 in *Central Themes in Biblical Theology: Mapping Unity in Diversity.* Grand Rapids, MI: Baker Academic, 2007.

Walvoord, John F. *The Revelation of Jesus Christ.* Chicago: Moody Press, 1966.

Wiarda, Tim. "Revelation 3:20: Imagery and Literary Context." *Journal of the Evangelical Theological Society* 38.2 (June 1995): 203–212.

Williams, Travis B. "The Divinity and Humanity of Caesar in 1 Peter 2,13." *Zeitschrift für die neutestamentliche Wissenschaft und die Kunde der älteren Kirche.* 105 (2014): 131–147.

Winslow, Donald. "Religion and the Early Roman Empire." Pages 237–254 in *The Catacombs and the Colosseum: The Roman Empire as the Setting of Primitive Christianity.* Eds. Stephen Benko and John J. O'Rourke. Valley Forge, PA: Judson, 1971.

Witherington, Ben, III. *Revelation.* New Cambridge Bible Commentary. Cambridge: Cambridge University Press, 2003.

Wong, Daniel K. K. "The Hidden Manna and the White Stone of Revelation 2:17." *Bibliotheca Sacra* 155 (April 1998): 346–354.

Wood, Leon. *A Commentary on Daniel.* Grand Rapids, MI: Zondervan, 1973.

Woods, Andrew M. "John and the Rapture: Revelation 2–3." Pages 195–224 in *Evidence for the Rapture: A Biblical Case for Pretribulationism.* Ed. John F. Hart. Chicago: Moody, 2015.

World Atlas. "Suicide Rates by Country." No pages. Cited 22 October 2016. Online: http://www.worldatlas.com/articles/countries-with-the-most-suicides-in-the-world.html.

Wright, N. T. "Jesus' Resurrection and Christian Origins." *Stimulus: The New Zealand Journal of Christian Thought and Practice* 16.1 (Feb 2008): 41–50.

———. *The Challenge of Jesus: Rediscovering Who Jesus Was and Is*. Downers Grove, IL: InterVarsity, 1999.

Also from **Energion Publications**

This book is a plea to return to biblical Christianity; Christianity that treasures and proclaims that Jesus died for us and consequently that we should take up our crosses and follow Him.

Amazon.com review

The primer allows the reader to gain a basic understanding of the need for textual criticism in light of the many skeptical claims made by folks like Bart Ehrman.

Amazon.com Review

More from Energion Publications

Personal Study
Holy Smoke! Unholy Fire	Bob McKibben	$14.99
The Jesus Paradigm	David Alan Black	$17.99
When People Speak for God	Henry Neufeld	$17.99
The Sacred Journey	Chris Surber	$11.99

Christian Living
Faith in the Public Square	Robert D. Cornwall	$16.99
Grief: Finding the Candle of Light	Jody Neufeld	$8.99
Crossing the Street	Robert LaRochelle	$16.99
Life in the Spirit	J. Hamilton Weston	$12.99

Bible Study
Learning and Living Scripture	Lentz/Neufeld	$12.99
Inspiration: Hard Questions, Honest Answers	Alden Thompson	$29.99
Colossians & Philemon	Allan R. Bevere	$12.99
Ephesians: A Participatory Study Guide	Robert D. Cornwall	$9.99

Theology
Christian Archy	David Alan Black	$9.99
The Politics of Witness	Allan R. Bevere	$9.99
Ultimate Allegiance	Robert D. Cornwall	$9.99
From Here to Eternity	Bruce Epperly	$5.99
The Journey to the Undiscovered Country	William Powell Tuck	$9.99
Eschatology: A Participatory Study Guide	Edward W. H. Vick	$9.99
The Adventist's Dilemma	Edward W. H. Vick	$14.99

Ministry
Clergy Table Talk	Kent Ira Groff	$9.99
Thrive	Ruth Fletcher	$14.99
Out of the Office: A Theology of Ministry	Bob Cornwall	$9.99

Generous Quantity Discounts Available
Dealer Inquiries Welcome
Energion Publications — P.O. Box 841
Gonzalez, FL_ 32560
Website: http://energionpubs.com
Phone: (850) 525-3916

www.ingramcontent.com/pod-product-compliance
Lightning Source LLC
LaVergne TN
LVHW041626070426
835507LV00008B/476